NEAL-SCHUMAN

WEBMASTER

LISA CHAMPELLI and
HOWARD ROSENBAUM

NEAL-SCHUMAN NETGUIDE SERIES

Neal-Schuman Publishers, Inc.
New York London

Published by Neal-Schuman Publishers, Inc.
100 Varick Street
New York, NY 10013

Printed and bound in the United States of America.

Library of Congress Cataloging-in-Publication Data

Champelli, Lisa.
Neal-Schuman WebMaster / by Lisa Champelli and Howard Rosenbaum.
p. cm.—(Neal-Schuman Netguides)
Includes bibliographical references and index.
ISBN 1–55570–307–0
1. Library information networks—United States. 2. World Wide Web (Information retrieval system) 3. Web sites—United States—Design. I. Rosenbaum, Howard. II. Title. III. Series.
Z674.75.W67C48 1997
025.04—DC21 97–16026

Table of Contents

Acknowledgments vii
Figures ix

Preface **xi**
How to Use the CD-ROM xiv
What's on the CD-ROM? xv
Instructions for Using the CD-ROM xv
How to Open the CD-ROM xv

Introduction **xix**
Growth of the World Wide Web xix
Why Should Libraries Provide Public Access to the Internet? xx
Libraries Strive to Respond to the Demand for Internet Access xxii

Chapter 1: Designing the Library Web Site 1
Taking It to the Web 1
Setting Goals 2
Selecting an Organizational Scheme 3
Developing the Site 6
Design Questions 9
But Will I Have to Learn HTML and CGI? 9
So What Exactly Is HTML, Anyway? 11
What Do Industry Standards Mean to Web Page Designers? 16
Design Guidelines 17
Identification and Consistency, a.k.a: "Where am I?" Clues 17
Manageability 19
Legibility 20
Graphic Enhancements 21
Interactivity 23
Content Is King 23
The Value of Resource Guides 23
Methods for Organizing Web Resources 26

Chapter 2: Exploring Intellectual Freedom Issues **31**
Introduction 31
Regulating the Internet: Federal and State Legislation 32

Rating Systems and Filtering Software 36
Broader Intellectual Freedom Considerations 38
Free Speech 39
Privacy 41
Access 43
Intellectual Property 44
Conclusions 46

Chapter 3: Developing Internet Acceptable Use Policies 47

Introduction 47
What Is an AUP? 48
Why Is an AUP Important for Libraries? 50
Is Every Library AUP the Same? 51
AUPs in Academic Libraries 54
AUPs and School Libraries 57
Integrating AUPs with Existing Policies 58
Preserving Student Rights 62
AUPs and Public Libraries 66
What Should the AUP Cover? 75
An AUP Template 77

Chapter 4: Training Library Staff and Patrons on Internet Use 81

Introduction 81
Training for Librarians and Library Staff 82
Training for Patrons 86
Templates for Training Programs 88
Template for a Training Program for Patrons 89
Training Program Example #1 90
Training Program Example #2 96
A Training Template for Librarian-Trainers 101
Is Training Worth the Trouble? 102

Chapter 5: Looking to the Future: What's Next? 107

Introduction 107
Large Scale Changes: What's Coming Next? 109
Socio-Cultural Changes 110
Economic Changes 114
Technological Changes 116
Library Responses 118
What You Can Do to Keep Current 120
World Wide Web Sites 121
Computer Conferences 124
USENET Newsgroups 126

Chapter References & Notes 127

Credits 147

Appendix A: Text of the Communications Decency Act 151

Appendix B: References to Useful Materials 161
- Managing Web Sites 161
- Search Tools 162
- Training Materials 163
- UNIX Skills 165

Appendix C: New Users' FAQ 167

Appendix D: Frameset Translation 173

Index 175

Colophon 181

Acknowledgments

To Howard, who first taught me about the Internet, how to create a Web page, and inspired an interest in ensuring that intellectual freedom principles don't get lost in the tangle of new technology; thank you for sharing this project with me—and for your ever-present good humor which persists in the face of deadline and course load pressures. Dr. Rosenbaum is just one of the professors in Indiana University's graduate program in Library and Information Science who give their best to teaching while pursuing independent research.

My deepest gratitude to all my family members, friends, professors, and colleagues who provided support and encouragement in this endeavor. I owe a huge debt to the talented Children's Librarians and other co-workers at Monroe County Public Library, especially to MCPL's first "Web Czar," Chris Jackson, who generously shares his knowledge of computing and regularly challenges me to think carefully about library Internet policies and Web services.

And, always, to my husband, David Holian, who makes me laugh and makes me coffee and makes me think I can. Thank you.

~Lisa Champelli

Thanks to my coauthor, Lisa Champelli. It was your work on the "Internet Advocate," a great Web resource, that started all this. It's been a pleasure working on this project with you. Shall we get started on the next edition?

As always, my gratitude to Blaise Cronin for his support and advice over the years.

And finally, special thanks to my wife, Kathy Anderson: Your support throughout this project made the work much easier; the book has benefited immensely from your critical eye.

~Howard Rosenbaum

Special thanks to our editor, Charles Harmon, for his patience, faith, and commitment to protecting the right to read—and view.

Many thanks to Rick McMullen and other staff members at Indiana University's Center for Innovative Computing Applications for all their assistance in producing the CD-ROM.

Beyond the people specified here, we'd like to extend our gratitude to the librarians who share their thoughts and feelings about library practices and policies on the variety of library-related listservs and newsgroups, which provide an ongoing forum for the exchange of information and ideas.

~LC/HR

Figures

Figure 1.1	Example of a Home Page Divided into Two Parts	5
Figure 1.2	An Example of an Internet Resource Guide for Educators	25
Figure 1.3	Resource Guides Can Be Entertaining as Well as Informative	26
Figure 1.4	The BPL Index has been renamed the Librarians' Index to the Internet and moved to http://sunsite.berkeley.edu/Internet Index	28
Figure 3.1	Setting Internet Policy Is Challenging, but not Necessarily Humorless	54
Figure 3.2	The Newark Memorial High School Library Home Page Begins with an Online Tour	63
Figure 3.3	The Pre-Home Page of the Morton Grove Public Library Web Site Asks Patrons to Review and Accept Internet Usage Rules	68

Preface

As creators of bibliographies, pathfinders, visual displays, program handouts, and newsletter articles, librarians have always been information producers. Creating Web pages and developing library Web sites is a new and dynamic way for librarians to produce resources that help facilitate public access to varying sources of information—particularly those that reside on the Internet. This can be both an exciting and frustrating task involving major expenses for art and design, consultants, and staff time. The *Neal Schuman WebMaster* is a multimedia kit designed to help you: build or enhance your Web site; provide public access to the Internet; and develop solid workable plans quickly and inexpensively. The kit consists of a web-enabled CD-ROM and a book. Our goal was to combine the best attributes of book, CD-ROM, and Web formats to facilitate your development of library policies, Web sites, and Internet training modules which will further library goals and save librarians time.

The book concentrates on libraries' use of the World Wide Web because the Web continues to be one of the most popular means of accessing information on the Internet and because the Web also enables librarians to play an important role in producing guides to Internet resources, publicizing library services, and instructing patrons about the use and nature of networked information.

The CD-ROM contains the full text of library policies, complete training modules for patrons and staff, templates of actual library home pages, icons to jazz up those pages, and a wealth of other resources we've collected to save you time and money in designing your site. Best of all, the CD-ROM is a Web-enabled CD-ROM, meaning that it contains active links to a multitude of Web sites where you can quickly access even more resources.

The *WebMaster* is designed to be used as a multimedia package; the material contained on the CD-ROM is integral to the content we cover in the book. Instead of spending time and effort searching for policy examples or looking for good library Web pages to use as a model, you can use what's here—and the links we provide to other examples on the CD-ROM—as a foundation for building your own policies, training programs, and Web pages.

AUDIENCE

The development of the Internet and the increasing popularity of Internet resources such as the World Wide Web (WWW) have opened a whole new realm of information for librarians, challenging information professionals of all kinds to learn about this dynamic new medium and the service issues it raises. Although growth of the WWW has progressed rapidly since its release by computer specialist Tim Berners-Lee in 1991, this interactive communication system is still in its infancy and primed to be influenced by librarians with a long history of developing, organizing, and facilitating access to a variety of information resources. Already librarians in school, public, academic, and special libraries have made significant contributions to the development of the WWW, some examples of which are provided throughout this book and on the CD-ROM. Libraries of all types and sizes will find the resources included here to be useful.

Designed for librarians preparing to build—or in the early stages of developing—a library Web site or who are planning to provide public access to the Internet, the *Neal-Schuman WebMaster* assumes that you already have an Internet connection. If you are seeking information on how to obtain an Internet connection, you may first want to consult one of several books on this topic, such as Susan Estrada's *Connecting to the Internet* (O'Reilly & Associates, Inc., 1993) or Karen G. Schneider's *The Internet Access Cookbook: A Librarian's Commonsense Guide to Low-Cost Connections* (Neal-Schuman Publishers, 1996). For additional resources, see the "Chapter References & Notes" listing at the end of this book.

SCOPE

The Internet resources a library makes available to its patrons depends in part on the kind of Internet connection (dial-up or direct) the library has, the costs involved, and its reasons for providing Internet access. Although your library's Internet access may include the provision of e-mail accounts, the ability to telnet to remote computer systems and subscribe to Usenet newsgroups, the *Neal-Schuman WebMaster* emphasizes use of the World Wide Web and discusses how libraries can develop their own Web sites to facilitate patron access to the Internet.

HyperText Markup Language, or HTML: A system of creating and controlling the format of documents on the World Wide Web. HTML is a system of tags that enables you to place text and images and create links on your Web page.

Although we do provide instruction on learning the HyperText Markup Language (also known as HTML) you need to know to create Web pages, we do not broach programming or explain how to design original graphic images. Instead, we focus on the underlying principles that establish the foundation for an effective library Web site. Because individual levels of Internet access vary so much, we have tried to generalize appropriately and suggest additional resources when available that may provide more specific information.

We concentrate on libraries' use of the WWW because the Web continues to be one of the most popular means of accessing information on the Internet, and because it enables librarians to play an important role in producing guides to Internet resources, publicizing library services, and instructing patrons about the use and nature of networked information. By outlining the critical issues integral to the world of networked information affecting librarians and other information professionals, we aim to provide you with the essential knowledge and skills you'll need to manage library Web services. The topics we address include these major issues:

- **Design Guidelines**: What should your library Web site look like? How will you organize it? What kind of content will you include?
- **Intellectual Freedom**: What are some of the policy-oriented questions librarians face when they venture onto the Internet? How will you handle questions of access, free speech, privacy, copyright, and censorship in the electronic arena?
- **Internet Acceptable Use Policies**: What is an acceptable use policy and why is it important for libraries providing Internet access? Does every library need one? What should this policy cover?
- **Training Options**: Do you have a responsibility to teach staff members how to search the Web? Will you provide instruction for your patrons on how to use this new information resource? How will you go about it? What should a training program cover?
- **The Future of Internet and Libraries**: What's next? You now may feel prepared to provide Internet services, but the Internet keeps changing so quickly— how will you keep up with new developments? What information resources are available to help you stay current?

The chapters that follow integrate reports from academic and government institutions researching the impact of the Internet on libraries and include the comments and insights of librarians who already have grappled with many of the questions we raise. Examples of different library approaches to providing access to the Internet are interspersed throughout the book, and sample Internet Acceptable Use Policies, guides to Web resources, training tutorials, and an intellectual freedom presentation are included on the CD-ROM packaged with this book. We provide templates in this electronic format to give you easy access to the information and make it simple for you to adapt the files to your library's needs. Although the materials included on the CD-ROM are fully accessible as they are, the CD-ROM also features numerous hypertext links to Web-based resources. Viewing the CD-ROM with an Internet connection and Web browser open will permit you to connect directly with these Web resources, expanding your access to related information.

HOW TO USE THE CD-ROM

The contents of the CD-ROM mirror the contents of the book. From the Table of Contents page, you can link to any of the other main sections. A navigation table is provided at the bottom of each of the main sections, allowing you to move easily to any other section. The heading in the table that is not highlighted and appears gray indicates that you are currently in that section.

From each of the main sections, you can link to the pages included in that section. These pages are often examples of Web pages that were included on the CD-ROM with the permission of their creators. We did not alter these pages in any way, (except to ensure that the links continued to work properly) so clicking on hypertext links that appear on these pages may take you to Web sites off the CD-ROM, and you will have to use your browser's Back button to return to the main section page on the CD-ROM.

The one exception is the Bibliography section, which includes separate bibliography pages we created. Each page in this section contains a navigation table that will allow you to move to any other bibliography page as well as back to the main bibliography page. Most of the links on these pages will take you to sites off the CD-ROM. Clicking on the Web icon that appears on the left side of the navigational table will always take you back to the Table of Contents page.

There are items on this CD-ROM that you can freely download and alter for your own use. These include the library-related icons and templates for library Web pages in the Design section and the template for an Acceptable Use Policy in the Acceptable Use Policy section.

The other items included on this CD-ROM appear here for reference purposes and remain the property of the authors. If you wish to use them in any way, you should contact us for our permission and, when necessary, copyright clearance. The same is true of any of the remote Internet sites we link to from the CD-ROM. Unless the creator of a site specifically grants permission for others to duplicate the images or information provided, you should always contact the creator before copying materials for your own use.

What's on the CD-ROM?

In the "How to use this CD-ROM" section of the CD-ROM, you will find instructions for downloading the latest version of a Web browser, a description of how the CD-ROM is organized, and an explanation of the relationship between downloading items from the CD-ROM and downloading Internet resources.

In the "Designing a Library Web Site" section, you will find templates that you can download or copy and adapt to create your very own pages. There is a collection of icons that you can download and use on your pages. Finally, there are examples of library-related Internet resource guides.

In the "Acceptable Use Policies" section, you will find a sample AUP that you can download and use as a template for your own policy. This will need to be adapted depending on the type of library you are working in. There are also examples of AUPs and Internet or Computer Use policy statements gathered from school, public, and academic institutions.

The "Intellectual Freedom" section features a presentation on intellectual freedom issues raised by the establishment of Internet connectivity in public libraries.

The "Training Options" section provides Web pages that will help you learn HTML and pages that will show you examples of Web-based tutorials set up by libraries to help patrons learn about the Internet and the Web.

In the "Chapter Bibliographies" section, you will find all of the Web-based citations referred to in the book. In order to use this section, you will have to be running a Web browser and an Internet connection. Clicking on these links will take you to sites off the CD-ROM—remember to use your browser's Back button to return to the bibliography page.

The "Credits" section lists all of the people and organizations that contributed information to this project with links to their corresponding Web pages.

Instructions for Using the CD-ROM

This section gives you the step-by-step instructions for opening the CD-ROM. You will find a quick list of these steps inside the back cover of this book, near the CD-ROM, so you can refer easily to the procedure while you load the CD.

How to Open the CD-ROM

The CD-ROM has been designed to work with both Macintosh and IBM-compatible computers. If you have a CD-ROM drive and a Web browser on your computer, you will be able to navigate the contents of the CD-ROM effectively.

Start by placing the CD-ROM in the drive. Then follow the procedure in this section that corresponds to the type of computer you are using. (*Note*: Directions for opening the CD-ROM may vary slightly depending on the operating system you are using.)

PC Users:

1. Start your Web browser.
2. Open the File menu in the top left corner of your menu bar; select **Open File**. A window should appear, prompting you to choose a directory or folder.
3. Choose the CD-ROM drive (often this is drive D: or E:). A list of all files on the CD-ROM appears.

   Click on the first file, named **Abinitio.htm** (which is Latin for *from the beginning*) and select **Open**. This displays the opening page of the CD-ROM.

   Click **Table of Contents** to get started using the CD.

Macintosh Users:

1. Start your Web browser.
2. Open the File menu in the top left corner of your menu bar; select **Open File**.
3. When the next window appears, choose **Desktop**. The next window should display a CD icon.

   Click the CD icon to open it. The list of files on the CD appears.

   Click on the first file, named **Abinitio.htm** (which is Latin for *from the beginning*) and select **Open**. This displays the opening page of the CD-ROM.

   Click **Table of Contents** to get started using the CD.

An alternate way to open the CD-ROM files after loading the CD and opening your Web browser is simply to type **d://** into the locator window of the Web browser (substitute the drive letter of your CD-ROM for **d://** if your CD-ROM is a different letter) and press Enter. Then click on the top, or first file that appears, called **Abinitio.htm**.

The contents of the CD-ROM include hypertext files and images intended to be viewed through a Web browser. You may be able to open .htm files in your word processing program, but these will be static documents, revealing the html code that supports Web pages. It may be useful for you to view and save the templates included on the CD-ROM in this way, but we intended the contents of the CD-ROM to be viewed and easily navigated through a Web browser.

You do not have to be connected to the Internet in order to use the CD-ROM. However, because many of the hypertext links on the CD-ROM lead to sites on the Internet, this CD-ROM will be most useful when viewed from a computer that is connected to the Internet, enabling you to connect to remote sites. Most of the items included on the CD-ROM are dynamic Web sites which continue to be updated by their developers. They are included on the CD-ROM with the permission of the developers for your easy review. Beneath the link to materials located on the CD-ROM, we have listed the Internet address, or URL, for a page when available. If you are connected to the Net, this gives you the option of copying and pasting the URL into your Web browser and connecting to the most recent version of a site, assuming it is still available.

Please Note: All the links included on the CD-ROM were working as of April 30, 1997. Because of the ever-changing nature of the Web, however, some sites may have moved or changed in the time the has passed since this book was completed.

CONVENTIONS USED IN THIS BOOK

Throughout the *Neal-Schuman WebMaster*, we have used certain design and typographical conventions to help you easily locate and use the information you need. You will encounter the following items in this book:

- Margin notes are used to provide the definition of Internet terms you may not have seen before.
- In sections of the book that have additional examples and information on the CD-ROM, we use special design boxes to highlight the steps for getting to the information on the CD-ROM.
- Commands you select are indicated in **bold** type.
- An extensive "Chapter References & Notes" listing is provided at the end of the book, which includes notes and bibliographic references for every chapter. If you have a question or want to learn more about a study, report, or Web site mentioned in the text, look for additional information in the "Chapter References & Notes" listing by turning to the appropriate chapter and looking for the name of the author or sponsoring organization. The entries are arranged alphabetically within each chapter's section.

Introduction

GROWTH OF THE WORLD WIDE WEB

The scope of information on the Web is astounding, considering that the World Wide Web is not very old. Growth of the Internet—especially of the World Wide Web—has increased astronomically in the last four years, profoundly affecting business, publishing, and education industries, not to mention libraries, *especially* libraries. Libraries are continually challenged to adopt new information technologies and expand their patrons' information options. Access to the Internet through the engaging medium of the WWW provides libraries with the opportunity to do just that. Although many libraries are still acquiring the means to connect to the Internet, hundreds of school, public, and academic libraries around the country have started providing student and public access to the Internet. They are realizing that librarians can and should play a central role in incorporating Internet access into library services and educating their patrons about this new information technology.

The Internet, a global network of computer systems, was created in the late 1960s by the United States Defense Department as an experimental method for sustaining communications across divergent computer networks. Public awareness of the Internet, also known as the *information superhighway*, increased dramatically in 1993 soon after the National Center for Supercomputing Applications freely distributed the first graphical Web browser, Mosaic, for both Windows and Macintosh computers. In a December 1993 *New York Times* article, Mosaic was described as the "killer application" of network computing, "a map to the buried treasures of the Information Age," and "the first window into cyberspace." It was quickly downloaded by hundreds of thousands of Internet users (especially computer scientists, librarians, software developers, and magazine publishers), eager for an easier way to find and retrieve information on the Internet.

Web Browser: A program you can use to view and navigate among Web documents.

The following year, Marc Andressen, creator of Mosaic, founded Netscape Communications Corporation and in October 1994 introduced the most popular Web browser to date, Netscape, and made it freely available to individual, academic and research users. Later Netscape Communications added public libraries and other nonprofit charitable organizations to its list of institutions eligible to download Netscape products for free. Internet Explorer, the Web browser from Microsoft Corporation, also is available free of charge.

The availability of these easy-to-use, graphical Web browsers fostered new interest in the Internet, which was growing at a rapid rate. Internet domain surveys indicate that between January and July of 1994, one million new hosts were added to the Internet. But it was the exploding number of World Wide Web hosts that most graphically depicted the skyrocketing nature of Internet use. "The Web has grown very fast. In fact, the Web has grown substantially faster than the Internet at large, as measured by number of hosts," reports Matthew Gray of the Massachusetts Institute of Technology. In June of 1993, a few months after the first test version of the Mosaic Web browser was introduced, there were 130 Web sites (http documents beginning with a unique hostname). By December 1994, two months after the release of Netscape, more than 10,000 Web sites were online. By June 1996, there were an estimated 230,000 Web sites on the Internet, according to Gray's *Web Summary*. The numbers continue to increase. In a survey of host names providing an http (or Web) service, Netcraft, a networking consultancy that specializes in Internet research and services, received responses from 135,396 Web servers in March 1996, from 462,047 in December 1996, from 739,706 sites in February 1997, and from more than one million sites in April 1997.

Web Site: A Web page or collection of pages created by individuals, libraries, businesses, or organizations and posted on the World Wide Web.

Although the January 1997 survey conducted by Network Wizards, a computer and communications company which produces the twice-yearly *Internet Domain Survey*, indicates that the Web continues to grow in size, it cautions: "In summary, it is not possible to determine the exact size of the Internet, where hosts are located, or how many users there are." The Internet Society, a non-governmental organization that works for the global coordination of the Internet, also reminds: "The Internet is a very complex, dynamic, distributed aggregation of more than 50 thousand autonomous networks. It defies definitive measurement." Nevertheless, numerous agencies continue to try and measure the Internet and count its users.

WHY SHOULD LIBRARIES PROVIDE PUBLIC ACCESS TO THE INTERNET?

Although estimates of the numbers of people in the United States who use the Internet range from 9.5 to 25 million and more, surveyors consistently note that Internet users typically are upscale professionals who use the Internet in the workplace or who can afford home access. The largest portion of nonprofessionals who use the Net are college students, using access provided by their academic institutions. These demographic characteristics have spurred many individuals and organizations to advocate for increased public access to the Internet, to help decrease divisions between the information haves and have-nots.

In his article, "The Internet and the Poor," Richard Civille, Executive Director of the Center for Civic Networking, states, "Internet access is important but does not in itself begin to divide classes of people. However, when the Internet suddenly becomes more useful—a personal research library—access politics assume new importance. Those who lack access will be left even further behind, and more rapidly so than ever before."

"Falling Through the Net: A Survey of 'Have-Nots' in Rural and Urban America," a study conducted by the U.S. Department of Commerce in 1995, found that poor people usually live in areas lacking the telephone lines needed for connecting to the Internet (not to mention their inability to purchase modems and other needed computer equipment). The national report urged "traditional providers of information access for the general public—the public schools and libraries" to help bridge the technology gap:

> These and other 'community access centers' can provide, at least during an interim period, a means for electronic access to all those who might not otherwise have such access. Policy prescriptions that include public 'safety nets' would complement the long-term strategy of hooking up all those households who want to be connected to the NII.

Even with the technological capabilities in place to provide universal access to the Internet, the costs involved still will prohibit access for many, observed Carole Henderson, Executive Director of the American Library Association's Washington Office. For this reason alone, the public library should "provide the electronic equivalent of one of its traditional functions—to provide access to a wide variety of information sources and viewpoints regardless of a user's economic status or research skills." In addition to providing equitable access, Henderson points out that public libraries also have the capabilities to "provide unique network information resources; offer training and assistance to the public; open up the library as an electronic doorway to new sources of information and expertise; and provide an electronic reference desk."

LIBRARIES STRIVE TO RESPOND TO THE DEMAND FOR INTERNET ACCESS

In the last few years, all kinds of libraries, but especially public libraries, have been striving to respond to the pervasive and persistent growth of the Internet and manage the demand for access to this dynamic new medium, as these examples show:

- Academic and research libraries, which have the longest history of Internet access, have been restructuring their services to better support use of Internet resources, developing subject guides to Web sites and soliciting reference questions through the Web.
- The *1995 Survey of Advanced Telecommunications in U.S. Public Schools* cites an increase in the number of U.S. public schools with access to the Internet, from 35 percent in 1994 to 50 percent in 1995. Gleason Sackman's *Hotlist of K-12 Internet School Sites* indicates that there were more than 1,700 K-12 schools in the United States with Web sites as of February 1997.
- Findings from *The 1996 National Survey of Public Libraries and the Internet: Progress and Issues: Final Report* show that public libraries in the United States made impressive gains in connectivity, from 21 percent of public libraries in the U.S. connected to the Internet in 1994, to 44 percent in 1996; and have made steady improvements in the numbers of libraries providing their patrons with access to the Internet: from 13 percent providing public access to the Internet in 1994, to 28 percent in 1996, and to a projected 50 percent by March 1997.

The authors of the above report declare:

> Public libraries deserve congratulations and recognition for the strides they have made in connecting to the Internet and in moving onto the global information superhighway. Not only has there been a significant increase in connectivity, but public libraries are committing significant resources to support their information technology (IT) infrastructure, increasing the number and band-width of their connections to the Internet, and providing additional public access terminals for their communities to access the Internet directly. Many public libraries are rapidly embracing the global networked environment and are implementing strategies to provide networked information services to their patrons.

But along with the recent successes libraries have made in incorporating Internet access into their library services come needs for still greater improvements. Only 23.7 percent of public libraries providing public Internet access offer access to the World Wide Web via graphical Web browsers, according to *The 1996 National Survey of Public Libraries*. In contrast, 22.7 percent provide gopher-based public access services and 22.3 percent provide text-based Web services. The 1996 survey data also found that only 10.7 percent of public libraries maintain a Web site, the quality of which varies greatly. As library and information science experts Bertot, McClure, and Zweizig observe,

> Some Web sites have only a homepage with a picture of the library and its hours of operation. Others have extensive online services, access to their OPAC, online reference and referral services, and links to other Web sites. The public library community is only beginning to identify quality standards and criteria of excellence for assessing networked services and determining the degree to which these services meet community information needs.

The ability of libraries to develop noteworthy Web sites will improve as more and more librarians obtain the basic technical skills needed for producing and maintaining their own Web pages, as we discuss later in this book. Most likely, the quality of library Web sites will continue to vary with the computer equipment available to the library and the technical expertise of librarians and other staff members—along with the time they have to devote to Web development. But libraries should be charging their librarians—not just the automation technicians or the computer support staff—with the responsibility of developing Web-based resources and services, which librarians can use effectively to direct patrons to Internet resources, instruct them in use of the Internet, and promote library programs and policies.

A fact Henderson noted years ago is echoed by McClure and others: Providing access to the Internet is really only the first step for libraries—not the last. McClure explains:

> [C]onnecting libraries is not always the most important problem to address. Equally important are issues of educating the public on how to use the NII (the National Information Infrastructure) and developing a range of applications and uses that promote network literacy and enhance the educational system. An understanding of the policy issues affecting the use of the NII and a clarification of the policies that will be needed to promote the use and impact of the NII are also essential.

The book addresses these issues by examining acceptable use policies, intellectual freedom principles, training considerations, and effective Web design guidelines for librarians looking to capitalize on the dynamic, interactive features of the Web and promote public access to the Internet.

Charged with the responsibility of providing equal access to information, and devising new ways of distributing information, libraries are primed to develop applications of Internet technologies in the public's interest. And, as experienced information navigators, librarians are perfectly suited to instruct people about the Internet and guide their search for the information resource gems that reside amidst the wealth of materials available on the World Wide Web. Called to the challenge, librarians cannot afford to pass up the exciting service opportunities that the Internet presents.

To connect to the Web sites and documents mentioned in this chapter, follow these steps:

1. Connect to the Internet.
2. Open the *WebMaster* CD-ROM.
3. On the Table of Contents page, click **Chapter Bibliographies**.
4. Click **Introduction**.

For a list of works cited in this chapter and additional references for more information, see the "Chapter References & Notes" listing at the end of this book.

Chapter 1

Designing the Library Web Site

TAKING IT TO THE WEB

As creators of bibliographies, pathfinders, visual displays, program handouts, and newsletter articles, librarians have always been information producers. Creating Web pages and developing library Web sites is a new and dynamic way for librarians to produce resources that help facilitate public access to varying sources of information—particularly those that reside on the Internet.

This chapter looks at how librarians can transfer their skills for organizing and producing information to effective Web page development. It also describes some of the new skills and knowledge needed for working in this digital medium and introduces basic design guidelines for creating Web sites. Courses in library and information science cover in-depth several of the topics broached in this chapter (strategies for organizing information, user needs, Web design, etc.). The intent here—assuming you already have access to a Web server, have established an account for the library with an Internet domain name, and have a place to store your files—is to provide an introduction to some of the issues libraries face when building a Web presence, along with examples of how various libraries have chosen to design their sites and the kind of content they include. Resources for learning more about Web design and the other topics introduced here are included in the "Chapter References & Notes" listing at the end of the book and on the CD-ROM.

As you learn in Chapters 2 and 3, there are several important issues to consider when you are designing a Web site for your library. Intellectual freedom issues and the development of an Acceptable Use Policy for your library's Internet access are both important topics you should consider before putting your library on the Web.

Among the first things information providers must consider are these questions: Why are you producing this information, and who is it for (who is your audience)? Answering these questions before you begin developing your Web site can help you determine what content to include on your site and the most effective way for organizing it. As with any library activity, knowing your audience is essential.

SETTING GOALS

In his book *HTML & CGI Unleashed*, communications expert John December provides a detailed checklist for Web planners, which recommends identifying user needs and defining the overall purpose and specific objectives for the site. The Morton Grove Public Library (MGPL) in Illinois incorporated this advice (and that of other Web developers and consultants) by establishing goals for its site. On a page titled "About the MGPL Web Site," it states:

> Our Web site was developed with three goals in mind:
> 1. To locate and provide easy access to Web sites for the Library's Reference staff, for use in providing reference service to Library patrons.
> 2. To provide an informative, easy-to-use introduction to the Web for Library patrons using in-house Internet workstations.
> 3. To make Library resources available outside the Library via the Internet, to Library patrons, other north suburban libraries, and the entire Internet community.

These goals list common reasons libraries develop Web sites. Clearly stating the goals for your site will help guide the content and organization scheme you choose.

So why are you developing a Web site for your library? Resist the temptation to establish a site simply because everyone else is! There's too much work involved in creating and maintaining a site to venture into it carelessly. The Web site you build and present to the world should reflect your library's mission—not your friend's library, or your grandma's library, or a flashy trend. (This is not to say, however, that you can't get some great ideas by paying attention to what your friend's library has done and by keeping up with the latest trends.)

If you simply want people searching the Web to know that you exist, you can create a single home page with the name and location of your library and leave it at that. But if your aim is to take full advantage of the Web's interactive capabilities, and you want people outside the library to know what resources reside inside the library and to be able to access some of those resources; or if you want to assist both internal and external users of your library with locating information that resides on the Internet, the next step is to outline the content you intend to provide on your Web site. This might include information about the library's collection, services, programs and special resources. Do you want to make bibliographies available on the Web site? Will you post a calendar of events? Will you offer reference assistance?

Determining what information you want to provide and how to present it is perhaps the most difficult step in preparing a publication of any kind for a general audience. Working in a hypertext environment makes this even more difficult because your organizational options multiply. In addition, libraries must consider not just the information they have to share, but what information their patrons want and need—and where they will expect to find it. To help visualize the overall structure of the Web site they'd like to create, some Web developers begin with a storyboard. The *storyboard* serves as a rough outline or draft of the layout for the Web site that shows the relationship of one Web page to another. Some people use index cards or single sheets of paper to represent individual Web pages; others create an outline on the computer. The point is to have something that you can easily move around and revise as you plan how to organize the information you want to include on your Web site. Sketching or diagramming how you will link different pieces of information may seem like extra work, but creating a storyboard before you construct your site can be a big timesaver.

Storyboard: An outline or draft of a Web site.

SELECTING AN ORGANIZATIONAL SCHEME

The way libraries have chosen to structure their Web sites is as varied as the design of their physical buildings. Some libraries have tried to duplicate the organizational divisions of their physical library on their Web site, assuming that people who are regular users of the library and familiar with how its resources are organized will be able to transfer that understanding to the Web site. For example, the home page of the Provo City (Utah) Library states:

> We have tried to organize the information the same way that it would appear in a public library. To go to a particular area of our library, just click on anything that is highlighted or underlined. So . . . use the buttons at the left to wander around and have a look.

Visitors to this site can "wander around" by selecting from a menu of navigational buttons that consistently appear on the left side of the library's web pages. From the Home Page of the Provo City Library, button options include: People, Friends, Facilities, Departments, Catalogs, Search, Fun, Local Utah, Federal.

As of April 1997, the Provo City Library was renovating its web site and adding more description of library resources and services, but the site still consisted largely of links to Internet resources. Some library sites divide the dual functions of their library's Web site (to describe the actual library and its resources and to facilitate access to Internet resources) by splitting the site into information found within the library and information accessible only through the Internet. The Morton Grove Public Library (MGPL) explicitly states this objective on its home page:

> Our site is divided into two parts: Library and Community Information, which includes information on Library events, policies, collections, etc.; and the Online Ready Reference System, which includes extensive reference information from the Library as well as links to WWW sites around the world.

The Boulder (Colorado) Public Library divides its home page (http://bcn.boulder.co.us/library/bpl/home.html) into links leading to "General Library Information" and links that make up the "Boulder Public Virtual Library." But it also nicely integrates the two divisions. For example, the Children's Library option under "General Library Information" includes a link to "Cyber Stacks for Kids," which appears as one of the main menu items in the Virtual Library section.

The Houston (Texas) Public Library (http://sparc.hpl.lib.tx.us/) offers four clearly defined menu options on its home page: "Internet Use Policy," "About the Library," "Internet Resources" and the

Figure 1.1
Example of a Home Page Divided into Two Parts

"Houston Public Library Catalog." Other libraries provide more direct links from their home page to information on their Web site. The Seattle (Washington) Public Library (http://www.spl.lib.wa.us) for instance includes more than 25 menu options under four main headings: "Library Services," "Online Resources," "Library News," and "More about the Library" as well as five separate links to "Locations & Hours," "Library Catalog," "Library Cards," "Search Help," and "New Pages." In addition to providing multiple menu options for accessing information on its own site, the Mount Arlington (New Jersey) Public Library (http://www.gti.net/mountarlington/) features several direct links from its home page to notable community Web sites, such as a site about the first dinosaur skeleton discovered in New Jersey.

Although the 1996 National Survey of Public Libraries and the Internet found that only 10.7 percent of public libraries maintain a Web site, the numbers of public library Web sites increase every year, and are easily accessed through several listings of libraries on the Web. Thomas Dowling's "libweb" list of Library Servers via the WWW indicates that more than 450 Academic Libraries (in the United States) have Web sites. And the list of School Library Pages in the United States, maintained by School Library Media Specialist Linda Bertland, features more than 300 school libraries with Web sites. Reviewing how other libraries have structured their Web sites will give you a chance to explore different organizational schemes and help generate ideas for how you would like to organize your own library's Web site.

To view these library Web sites and lists of libraries on the Web, follow these steps:

1. Connect to the Internet.
2. Open the *WebMaster* CD-ROM.
3. From the Table of Contents, click **Chapter Bibliographies**.
4. Choose **Design Guidelines**.

Is there a "best" way to organize the information presented on your Web site? Yes. The best way is the way that makes the most sense to your users. Ideally, site developers should survey prospective users about the kinds of information they would like included on the site and then test the site with sample users as it's being developed. Once the site is up, solicit feedback through your Web pages, pay attention to questions people ask as they try to navigate the site, and note recurring problems, complaints, and suggestions. The following section describes how the Monroe County Public Library (MCPL) in Bloomington, Indiana, designed its site.

DEVELOPING THE SITE

The MCPL Web site initially was developed by members of Indiana University's "Public Web Project" course (taught by Dr. Thom Gillespie at Indiana University's School of Library Information Science), working closely with MCPL Reference/Automation Librarian Christopher Jackson. In consultation with Jackson and several other librarians who volunteered to help, the MCPL Web site was originally designed with the outside user as the focus audience. This was decided partly because the library had not yet begun to provide public access to the Internet and partly to concentrate on designing a site that would make sense to people who were not familiar with the actual library, its layout, or its services.

After brainstorming descriptions of different library users and the kinds of information they sought, the developers debated different ways of organizing the information to be included on the site. Their initial design featured four main categories, with examples of the kinds of information that would be found within those categories:

- About the Library
  hours, map, administration . . .
- Calendar of Events
  storytelling, tutor help, writing workshops . . .
- Departments and Services
  fiction, children, circulation . . .
- Searchable Resources
  OPAC (Online Public Access Catalog) CD-ROM Database . . .

Once an organizational structure was in place, class members created a paper prototype of the site and tested how easy it was for users to determine how to find answers to sample questions, such as

1. When will the next story hour for children be held?
2. What is the maximum number of books you can check out?

According to Jackson, testing revealed that this initial design, based on the library's departmental structure, was confusing to members of the public who didn't know what to expect from headings titled "Reference," "Circulation," "Indiana Room," etc. Consequently, the developers revised the design to incorporate a more cognitive model of the library and tested this second version:

- About the Library
  Hours , Maps, Facilities . . .
- Calendar of Events
  Booksales, Children's Programs, This Week at the Library . . .
- Collections
  Fiction, Non-Fiction, Audio-Visual, Children's . . .
- Services
  Circulation, Programs, Bookmobile . . .
- Searchable Resources
  Library Catalog, Community Organizations, WWW Resources . . .

The second usability test indicated that users found the revised structure easy to navigate and nearly all the sample questions were easily answered.

"This is, in my opinion," says Jackson, "the most valuable lesson (and benefit) from the entire project: you can't assume what makes sense to users; you must test, and you must be ready to abandon approaches that testing proves ineffective. Working in a library, we are unable to envision how our institution is perceived by the average patron."

Satisfied with the results, the class members realized that although the site was designed specifically for the Monroe County Public Library, it was actually a template—a site that any public library could implement with only minor modifications because the class members had focused on developing the shell of the Web site's structure, but not the content of individual pages.

The prototype structure of the MCPL site is included on the CD-ROM. To use the structure, follow these steps:

1. Open the CD-ROM and select the **Table of Contents** page.
2. Click **Designing a Library Web Site**.
3. Select **Template for a Library Web Site**.
4. You can save these Web pages as html (or .htm) files to a word processing program on your computer in order to revise the contents with information specific to your own library. Save the files in an ASCII format with an html file extension.
5. Use a file transferring program to move the files into your library's Web directory. Check with your systems administrator for details about how to do this.

MCPL installed the tested Web site on its own server with the understanding that it was (as most Web sites are) a work in progress and would most likely evolve. The next phase of development concentrated on adding content to the site. As members of different departments within the library (Reference, Children's, and the Indiana Room) began describing their department's collections, services and programs, they couldn't help but emphasize the needs of the people they most frequently serve—the patrons who regularly come *into* the library to receive information.

Consequently, the content developers of the MCPL site—MCPL librarians—focused on the inside user as the main audience and suggested organizing some information departmentally. Although adding links to individual library departments would enable patrons familiar with those departments to find them easily on the Web, organizing information this way also benefited the librarians producing and maintaining information about their department for the Web site. It was simply easier to manage the information that pertained to a department by having it all link to a departmental home page.

One of the many advantages of hypertext, however, is that it allows for a number of ways to access information. Content developers were careful to keep the original organizational shell of the site intact, preserving the overall focus on the needs of the remote or outside user, by linking information they created back to one of the five main categories that appear on MCPL's home page menu. The current home page for MCPL includes a link to "departments" beneath the top heading "About the Library." To visit the MCPL home page, see http://www.monroe.lib.in.us/.

In general, just as the library builds its collection to serve and reflect community interests, a library's Web site should be designed to serve the local user. But it should also remember its remote audience and strive to make sense to people who will be accessing the site from outside the library. Once your site is on the Web, it may be viewed by people from around the world who have never set foot in your library—and never will. If the information you provide is clearly labeled and described, it will at least be understandable, and perhaps, of use, as well.

DESIGN QUESTIONS

This section provides the answers to basic questions you may have as you begin designing your library Web site.

But Will I Have to Learn HTML and CGI?

Although development of your library's Web site may begin with one or two people, adding to and maintaining the site will most likely evolve into a group effort. Ideally, designing a large-scale Web site should be a collaborative project conducted by people with different skills, advises designer Darrell Sano. In his book *Designing Large-Scale Web Sites: A Visual Design Methodology*, he recommends the design team include:

> A computer programmer familiar with Internet technology, database architecture, CGI scripting and Java; a visual designer and user interface designer who understand designing interactive applications and how to organize and structure large infor-

> mation projects, an editor and writer should be familiar with hypertext online documentation, search engines and query methods; and a marketer who understands the power of the Net.

Certainly, Sano's advice is geared more toward developers of commercial Web sites than small to mid-size libraries who may have only a few people on staff interested in learning HTML (HyperText Markup Language) and willing to take on maintenance of the library Web site or selected pages in addition to their other responsibilities. But Sano's advice points out that depending on the skills of the developers, library Web sites will employ varying degrees of technology.

At the very least, you will need to learn the basic standards of HTML. But although you should understand what CGI (Common Gateway Interface) is and what it can do, you do not have to learn this programming language in order to create effective Web pages. For librarians with the time and patience to learn CGI, Perl, Java, and other programming languages that capitalize on the interactive capabilities of the Web, there are many print and Web resources listed in the "Chapter References & Notes" section at the end of the book that can help you learn these advanced skills. Also, as designers have made icons and images available on the Web free of charge, many Web developers have made their programming scripts for forms available for others to use. (See "Matt's Script Archive," for example, available at http://worldwidemart.com/scripts/.) But there's no need to be intimidated by the sight of forms, image maps, and animated images. Anyone with the desire to learn the rules for writing standard HTML and some basic design principles can create interesting, entertaining, and useful Web sites.

Further information about CGI is available on the CD-ROM. Use the following steps to access it:

1. From the Table of Contents, click **Training Options**.
2. Click **HTML Demonstration Pages**.
3. Scroll down and select **Forms**.

To find the link to Matt's Script Archive and other sites that can help you learn more advanced Web development skills, go back to the Table of Contents page.

1. Click on **Chapter Bibliographies** and then choose **Design Guidelines**.
2. At the top of the Bibliography for Design Chapter page, click the link for **Learning HTML, Image Maps and Forms**. Matt's Script Archive and related sites appear near the end of the section.

So What Exactly Is HTML, Anyway?

HTML, or Hypertext Markup Language, is the set of standard codes or "language" used to create Web documents. It enables Web browsers to display text formatted with HTML in a readable form, no matter what kind of browser is being used (Lynx, Internet Explorer, Mosaic, Netscape, etc.) or what kind of operating system (DOS, Macintosh, Windows 95) is running the browser. The HTML must conform, however, to certain standards established by the World Wide Web Consortium (W3C), an international organization of member agencies dedicated to promoting the evolution and interoperability of the Web.

You write HTML code with any kind of program that can save your text in a plain text format called *ASCII* (American Standard Code for Information Interchange). Some designers first write the content of the Web pages with a word processing program like Microsoft Word or WordPerfect and include the HTML codes at this stage. Others prefer to start a file in their Web directory and write the text and add the HTML codes using their Web server's text editor (such as Pico). Various software programs, called *HTML editors*, are available now that make it easier to write HTML code by enabling you to click on an icon to insert different HTML tags. Newer versions of traditional word processing programs also include features for generating HTML code. The latest version of Microsoft Word, for example, includes a toolbar button for inserting hyperlinks in your text. Software programs also are available that can automatically convert word processing documents into HTML text.

ASCII: A file format that saves documents in plain text with no formatting. Most programs have some method of reading files saved in an ASCII format.

HTML Editor: A type of software program designed to help you write and edit documents using HTML.

Although far from perfect, these tools are worth investigating further. Find lists of HTML editors on the CD-ROM by following these steps:

1. From the Table of Contents, click **Chapter Bibliographies**.
2. Click **Design Guidelines**.
3. Click **HTML Editors and Link Checkers**.
4. Click the link of the document you want to see.

Just as many word processing programs have a menu option for displaying the typesetting codes that format a document (such as the font size, hard returns, line spacing, etc.), most Web browsers have an option enabling you to see what the HTML code for a Web document looks like. In Netscape, open the View menu and choose **Document Source**. This reveals the HTML codes embedded in the document displayed on the browser screen. In Lynx, the text-only

Web browser, the \ (backslash) key alternately displays the HTML code (the source view) and the formatted view of a Web document.

Taking a Look at HTML Code

Looking at the source code of various Web pages can help you learn what different HTML codes you can use to format text. The following example shows you the HTML code for the MCPL home page:

```
<HTML>
<HEAD>
<TITLE>Template for Library Home Page</TITLE>
</HEAD>
<BODY>
<BODY BGCOLOR="FFFFFF">
<center><H1>Monroe County Public Library Home</H1></center>
<ul>
<li><A HREF="aboutpwp.htm"><B>About the Library</B></A> <br>
<font size=-1> Hours, Maps, Facilities ... </font>
<p>
<li>
<A HREF="calendar.htm"><B>Calendar of Events</B></A> <br>
<font size=-1>Booksales, Children's Programs,
This Week at the Library ...</font>
<p>
<li><A HREF="collect.htm"><B>Collections</B></A>
<br><font size=-1>
Fiction, Non-Fiction, Audio-Visual, Children ...</font>
<p>
<li><A HREF="services.htm"><B>Services</B></A>
<br><font size=-1>
Circulation, Programs, Bookmobile ...</font>
<p>

<li><A HREF="serchabl.htm"><B>Searchable Resources</B></A>
<br><font size=-1>
Library Catalog, Community Organizations, WWW Resources ...</font>
</ul>
<hr>
<center>
<font size=+1>I</font>ndex |
<font size=+1>A</font>sk A Librarian</a> |
<font size=+1>H</font>elp</a> </center>
<hr>
</BODY>
</HTML>
```

You will notice that HTML consists of a variety of "paired" and "unpaired" tags. Paired codes typically look something like this:

<HTML CODE> Formatted Text </HTML CODE>

Paired Tags: HTML codes that have a beginning tag and an end tag.

The HTML code must appear within brackets (< >). Paired codes have a beginning tag, which turns on the specified formatting feature (such as font size, bold, or indents, etc.) and the corresponding closing tag, preceded by a slash, which turns the feature off. Unpaired tags do not have an end tag. The tag indicating a line break, for example, <BR>, is an unpaired tag that does not have a closing partner.

Unpaired Tag: An HTML tag that does not require a closing tag.

To comply with the most basic levels of HTML, all Web documents should contain the following paired tags:

<HTML> </HTML>	The opening part of this tag appears at the start of your document to inform Web browsers that this is an HTML document. The closing tag appears at the end of the document.
<HEAD> </HEAD>	The header tag appears immediately after the <HTML> tag to indicate that the following section of the document contains information, such as the document's title, that should not be displayed by the browser.
<TITLE> </TITLE>	Text inserted between the opening and closing TITLE tags will appear in the very top section of the browser screen to indicate the title of your document.
<BODY> </BODY>	The BODY tag defines the text area, or the heart, of your document. The opening BODY tag follows the closing HEAD tag; the closing BODY tag appears right before the closing HTML tag.

These standard HTML tags would appear in the following way:

```
<HTML>
<HEAD>
<TITLE> Your Basic Web Page </TITLE>
</HEAD>
<BODY>
Text describing your basic Web page appears here.
</BODY>
</HTML>
```

You can display a Web page using only these basic HTML tags, but the real fun part of creating a Web page is linking it to other Web documents by using hypertext and inserting images in your document. The HTML code for linking to another document includes an A, usually known as the anchor tag, and HREF, short for Hypertext REFerence, plus the file name or URL (Uniform Resource Locator) of the document you want to access. The link looks like this:

```
<A HREF="http://homepage.html"> Home Page </A>
```

The text between the opening and closing anchor tags becomes the hypertext, or the highlighted words that users will select to access the linked document. The HTML code for displaying images in a Web page is an unpaired tag that basically looks like this:

```
<IMG SRC="graphic.gif">
```

More detailed explanations of various HTML tags, their functions and special attributes, are provided on the CD-ROM. Follow these steps:

1. From the Table of Contents, click **Training Options**.
2. Click the **HTML Demonstration Pages**.

See also Kevin Werbach's "Bare Bones Guide to HTML," by returning to the Table of Contents and clicking **Designing a Library Web Site**. Finally, click **Kevin Werbach's Bare Bones Guide to HTML**. The "Bare Bones Guide" lists all of the HTML tags that current versions of most browsers are likely to recognize, including all the tags in the HTML 3.2 specification, as well as Netscape extensions.

The WWW Consortium regularly considers proposals for new HTML codes to be included as standard HTML and sets new levels or versions of HTML. As of May 1996, the current standard in use was level 3.2 which added some "widely used features such as tables, applets and text flow around images, while providing backwards compatibility with the existing standard, HTML 2.0."

The HTML standards help ensure that Web documents will be accessible from a variety of computer platforms and browsers. Yet, the creators of Web documents continue to push for more advanced features, providing greater flexibility in page layout and other design techniques. Aiming to satisfy designers and attract more users to its browser, Netscape has continually added advanced features or extensions to standard HTML that are usually only viewable with the latest version of Netscape software. The FRAMES code is an example of such an extension.

Web documents that use the <FRAMES> paired tag can format text in distinct windows or frames on the screen. In addition to separating text in different boxes as it's possible to do with the <TABLES> element, the <FRAMES> tag allows for each frame to have its own scroll bar.

At the time of this writing, only Netscape 2.0 or above will display documents formatted as frames. Unless the document also includes a <NOFRAMES> tag and supporting code, no text will appear on screen if you are using a Web browser that does not understand the FRAMES code. This feature interferes with the universal aspect of HTML by preventing the display of text. Usually, if a browser does not understand a certain HTML tag, it will ignore the formatting code and display the text in any way it can. Some versions of Lynx browsers, for example, do not understand tables, but still manage to present text on screen to the viewer.

There are software tools and shareware programs available on the Web that can check to see that the HTML codes you have used in a Web page conform to standard specifications. These tools are called *HTML validators*. Some are stricter than others. There are other tools, called *link checkers* that can help detect whether any of the sites you link to have disappeared. To see a list of these tools and learn more about them, follow these steps:

1. Open the CD-ROM with your Internet connection running.
2. From the Table of Contents, click on **Chapter Bibliographies**.
3. Click on **Design Guidelines**.
4. On the Bibliography for Design Chapter page, click on the link for the "HTML Editors and Link Checkers" section.

What Do Industry Standards Mean to Web Page Designers?

The conscientious Web page designer will design for the lowest common denominator to ensure that all Web documents will appear in a legible format across all types and versions of browsers. Even if your library is running the latest version of Netscape, your patrons might have access only to a text-based browser from their homes or still be using an early version of Netscape or Internet Explorer. Designing for the lowest common denominator doesn't mean that you can't use the latest Netscape or Internet Explorer enhancements. Rather, you must be certain that all information provided in your document can be viewed on any number of different browsers. Thus, documents formatted in <FRAMES> must also employ the <NO FRAMES> tag. Images included in your document should include an ALT=" " element to describe the image for people using text-based browsers or who view Web pages with the graphics turned off. It's also possible for blind and visually impaired people to use the Web with adaptive technology that reads the contents of Web pages to them. For these reasons, it's important to use descriptive terms that will help the user interpret the graphical information. For example, if you have a graphic image at the top of your library's home page that gives the name of your library, you'll want to provide that information in the alt tag, as: ALT="[Name of Library"]. Remember to include the brackets because they signal to the user that this text replaces an image. But if the image on the page is simply decorative, the proper tag to use is ALT=" " with nothing in-between the quotes. This keeps the screen on text-based browsers from being cluttered with extraneous information.

Some Web pages offer the user different options for viewing pages (Text Only or No Frames), depending on the browser they are using or the speed of their modem. View your pages in as many different kinds of browsers as possible (or have others take a look for you and provide feedback), and make sure the information is legible. But don't spend a lot of time trying to make your pages look absolutely perfect for each browser. You simply cannot control how individual browsers and the preferences set on individual computer terminals may interpret the HTML code. HTML was created as a functional way to deliver information to different computer systems—it wasn't meant to be a design tool and doesn't offer designers detailed control over the layout and appearance of their pages. For this reason, many designers prefer to use image maps, which permit them to have greater control over how font size and style and the layout of elements on screen will appear to the user.

Image Map: An image map is a "clickable image" that enables you to use an entire image or portions of it as a link to other sites.

DESIGN GUIDELINES

Whether or not you have the ability to create original artwork for your site, following some basic design guidelines can help your page look good and make sense to people trying to use it. This section introduces some issues to consider as you work on the design of your library Web site.

Identification and Consistency, a.k.a: "Where am I?" Clues

For the designer who has spent hours creating and fine-tuning a series of pages for a Web site, linking one to the next, it seems obvious that the individual pages belong together and compose a whole. After labeling the home page with the name of the library, the date the page was created and the name of a contact person, designers sometimes make the mistake of omitting identifying information on following pages. Because visitors to your library's Web site may start on a page other than the library's home page, it's important to indicate on each page that it is part of your library's Web site and provide links for moving to the top level sections of the site.

To understand why this is important, consider the format of newspapers and magazines. At the top or bottom of most pages, you'll find the name of the publication, the issue date, and often a page number. Articles that are continued from one section of the publication to another state the page number where the article continues; the continued section usually notes the page from which the article is continued. Similarly, clearly labeling all your Web pages with the name of the library and providing hypertext links enables your users to determine where they have landed on the World Wide Web and move easily from one section of your site to another. Including the URL at the bottom of each page functions as a page number of sorts. These identifying elements and navigational links can also help establish a level of consistency for individual Web pages which may have been authored and designed by different people, but are all part of the library's Web site. They also help users realize when they have accessed information that was produced by the library and when they have linked to a page that was not developed by the library.

Some good examples of navigational and locator cues are found at the following library sites:

- St. Paul (Minneapolis) Public Library (http://www.stpaul.lib.mn.us/) explains on its home page that a blue dot next to a link signals that the link is to a site outside the library, whereas a red dot indicates pages maintained by the library.

- The Flint (Michigan) Public Library (http://www.flint.lib.mi.us/) features the library's logo in the upper-left corner of its Web pages. Thus, even when the pages change colors between departments, it's still apparent that the page is part of the library's Web site.
- A library card logo billing the Kansas City Public Library (http://www.kcpl.lib.mo.us/) as "the information playground" appears consistently at the bottom of its pages. The icon serves as a link back to the library's home page.
- Along with displaying its name and navigational buttons prominently at the top of its Web pages, the Evanston Public Library (http://www.evanston.lib.il.us/) features a distinctive banner on the left side of all of its pages.

Many libraries and other organizations establish style guides for designers of their Web pages, to ensure a consistent appearance and format for all pages. See these examples:

- IUB Libraries World Wide Web Information Providers Rights and Responsibilities
  <http://www.indiana.edu/~libcbrst/rights.html>
- U.S. Department of Education World Wide Web (WWW) Server Standards and Guidelines
  <http://inet.ed.gov/~kstubbs/wwwstds.html>
- US EPA Region 2: Ten Elements of Web Style
  <http://www.epa.gov/Region2/library/style.htm>
- Bellingham Public Schools—Designing School Home Pages
  <http://www.bham.wednet.edu/homepage.htm>

You may want to consider including these common identification elements on your library Web site:

- The name of your library or an identifying logo or other graphical element representing the library should appear on all pages comprising the library's Web site. Consider placing this element on the top of the page for easy recognition.
- An accurate title and header should be repeated throughout your site. Search engines and indexers will often categorize your site by its title and the first few lines of text that appear on the page. Giving your page a descriptive header will help users understand its purpose and the information it provides.
- Hypertext links that enable the user to move to other sections of your Web site help visitors move through the site easily. These links usually appear at the bottom of the page in order to con-

serve valuable "first screen" space, but sometimes appear at the top or sides of pages. Pages providing general information about the library or its Web site usually include the complete set of links to other sections on the site. Pages providing more specific information (such as booklists) usually link back to the "parent" section.

Make all hypertext links— especially navigational links— as descriptive as possible. "Back," "Next," and "Previous" don't mean much to someone who arrived in the middle of a set of pages. And "click _here_ for more information", doesn't let the user know what additional information to expect. If you're linking to a page titled "Mystery Fiction for Adults," ideally, your hypertext link should state Mystery Fiction for Adults.

- The date the page was created and last updated should be a repeating element. This helps the user determine the currency of information on the page and whether the page is still being maintained.
- The name of a contact person should appear on the page. Ideally, the contact name would be in the form of a "mailto" link, indicating who is responsible for the page and who users can contact to ask questions and provide comments.
- The URL of the page should be listed on the page. Although this information appears in the location window of the Web browser, including the URL at the bottom of the page is useful for people who may print out the Web page (and not have a printer that automatically stamps the URL on the printout) and need to cite or refer back to the page later.

Manageability

Although it certainly may be easier for the developer of a Web site to present information on a single long page—dividing the information you provide into separate pages helps the user comprehend the different topics you've identified. (Isn't it easier to get through a long book when it's broken down into short chapters?) Long pages—large files of information—also take longer to download and to appear on the user's computer screen. People trying to access your page with a slow modem may become impatient and decide your site isn't worth the wait. Long pages typically also require more use of the scroll bar. Novice computer users often don't realize that there is more information on a page than what appears on screen and don't know they should use the scroll bar to see the rest of the page. Including a long list of links on your home page, especially when that list appears below the first screenful of information, doesn't necessarily make that

Download: The process by which an electronic file is copied from a computer on the Internet to your personal computer.

information more accessible. Providing descriptive menu choices that indicate what other information appears on your site, does alert users to the range of information you provide.

Some Web developers will include a single file as an option for people who want to easily print out information that has been divided among several pages. If you do prepare pages with hypertext links that will be used as print reference sources, remember to list the URLs for each hypertext link to facilitate access to those sites from the print source.

Legibility

As much fun as it is to experiment with an "MTV style" of design, it doesn't make any sense to provide information on a Web page that is difficult to read. Two things in particular affect the legibility of your page: font size and style, and the combination of colors you use. Unless you're creating a picture or image map and inserting text from a graphics software program, basic HTML doesn't really give you any text style choices, except that the <FONT> tag makes text appear a little narrower. HTML allows you to specify font sizes from 1 (the smallest) to 7 (the largest). Of course, the smaller size font you use, the more text you can fit on a single screen — and the more difficult it is to read. The default font size in Netscape and Internet Explorer is 3. Consider using the next largest font size as the default font when creating pages specifically for new readers or the elderly. Larger sizes normally are reserved for titles and headers. Sizes smaller than 3 are usually used for identification elements, such as the page author, date and URL.

Perhaps the biggest hindrance to legibility is background color. You can specify the background pattern or color of a document using the <BODY BACKGROUND="image.gif"> tag or by indicating <BODY BGCOLOR="#RRGGBB"> and inserting one of the six character color codes. You also can specify the color of the text in your document and the color of hypertext links by using a different color to identify visited links and active links. As you would probably guess, dark text on a dark background color simply does not show up well. Yet, many Web page designers make this mistake—most likely because the blue background they choose appears sky blue on their computer screen, although the configurations for other computer screens may interpret the color as a midnight blue.

The only color code guaranteed to look the same on all computer screens is the code for white: <BGCOLOR="#FFFFFF">. However, if you want a little variation (and don't care how an individual terminal setting will interpret the color), in general, it's best to select contrasting colors. According to Faber Birren, author of *Color: A Survey in Words and Pictures*, (New York: University Books, 1963), black on yellow is the most legible combination, followed by green, red, or blue on a white background. Yellow text on a black background is the most illegible combination, although striking in appearance. A 1994 article in the *Journal of Performance and Instruction*, specified these effective color combinations to use on computer screens:

Background	Highlights	Foreground
white	dark blue	red, orange
light gray	blue, green, black	red
blue	light yellow, white	yellow, red
light blue	dark blue, dark green	red-orange
light yellow	violet, brown	red

In addition to being visually pleasing, the colors you choose can help separate one section of your site from another and may help users distinguish your site from others.

Resources to help you learn more about color codes appear on the CD-ROM. Follow these steps:

1. With your Internet connection running, open the CD-ROM and go to the Table of Contents.
2. Click on **Chapter Bibliographies** and then on **Design Guidelines**.
3. At the Bibliography for Design page, click on the link for the "Icons/Colors/Colors and Textures," and click your choice.

Graphic Enhancements

As discussed above, using images and icons for your site can also help create a consistent appearance across pages and function as navigational cues. Images also can help break up big blocks of text, making your page both easier to read and more visually pleasing. Designer William Horton, author of *The Icon Book: Visual Symbols for Computer Systems and Documentation*, lists several reasons for using icons: To help increase user recognition and recall, to conserve space, to limit the amount of reading users must do, and to help create a more universally understandable interface. He cautions, however, that icons by themselves are meaningless:

> Don't design icons to stand alone. An icon, like a word, achieves meaning only by its use in a particular context. Trying to make an icon completely unambiguous to everyone under all possible circumstances is usually impossible in most cases. Attempting such a feat leads to overly complex designs. Instead, design the icon so that under actual viewing conditions it combines with other information in the user's field of view and working memory to produce a clear meaning.

Horton advises selecting symbols "that naturally and directly suggest the idea you want to communicate. Try to show actual or familiar objects first, then consider more abstract symbols."

A wide variety of graphic design books and software programs are available to help you learn how to create your own images. You may find it easier to access one of the numerous Web sites that offer free icons for designers to use in their pages. Although it's also possible to "grab" any image from a Web page if you are using Netscape 1.1 and Internet Explorer 1.0 or higher, designers should remember that some images may be copyrighted and are not meant to be freely shared. Unless you retrieve the image from an archive clearly intended to share images freely, you must contact the owner of the image or page designer for permission to copy the icon.

Some common icons that may be useful to developers of library Web sites are included on the *WebMaster* CD-ROM for easy copying. Direct links to other icon archives also are provided on the CD-ROM and in the bibliography. Again, conscientious designers may want to limit the amount and size of images they use as a courtesy to people accessing the Web site with low-speed modems, or memory-challenged computers. The larger the image, the longer it will take to download—and, of course, images don't appear at all in documents viewed by text-only browsers.

To find the icons included on the CD-ROM, follow these steps:

1. Go to the Table of Contents and click on **Designing a Library Web Site**.
2. At the top of this page, click on the **link to icons**. This will take you down to another link called "Sample Icons."
3. Click on **Sample Icons** to move to the page of icons on the CD-ROM.

Interactivity

Whenever possible, capitalize on the interactive nature of the Web. If you're providing information about another organization or publication that has a Web site—link to it. Make it easy for your users to access primary information sources. Even including a simple "mailto" option on a page serves as a convenient way for patrons to communicate with information providers (assuming the "mailto" contact regularly checks his mail). Several libraries permit patrons to submit reference questions by using regular e-mail or by filling out a form on the library's Web page.

The Reading Public Library in Massachusetts uses forms on one of its Web pages that patrons can use to submit book reviews. It's also possible to search this site for particular reviews. See the Book Review Page from the Reading Public Library (http://www.netcasters.com/rpl/ booktop.html). The Spokane Public Library created a Web page called "Get-A-Clue" (http://splnet.spokpl.lib.wa.us/sr-clue.html) featuring Internet-related activities it incorporated into its 1996 summer reading program for children and teens. One of the activities encouraged kids who had attended an Internet Training session to find Web sites of interest to them by searching for sites that matched the "clue" for that week, such as "Find a Site that features information about Animals or Pets."

Content Is King

Although it may be the visual design of a page that first captures your attention, the thing that keeps people coming back is the information your site provides—the content. A principal designer for webreference.com, a Web Development company, Andrew King states:

> Original content is the most important trait of a great Web site. Sites that provide only links to other sites are essentially meta-lists, while sites that have some information that's useful to the user stand out and will be revisited. A recent check of webreference.com's statistics confirms this, my article HTML 3.0 and Netscape 3.0 gets nearly as many hits as the Table of Contents page. Content is King.

THE VALUE OF RESOURCE GUIDES

In addition to original content, sites that repackage information, organize it, and make it more accessible to a wide audience are also highly valuable. It's their experience with organizing information and producing pathfinders to information topics that make librarians ideal developers of Web-based guides to Internet resources. Louis Rosenfeld, vice president of Argus Associates, Inc., the Clearinghouse for Subject Resource Guides, notes:

> . . . most of the attempts to make the Internet's information more useable focus on the tangible efforts of non-librarians: improved retrieval technologies and better-designed user interfaces. However, the intellectual effort of value-added repackaging, a specialty of the information profession, may be of even greater importance to making the Internet a valuable information environment.

Started in 1993, the Argus Clearinghouse (http://www. clearinghouse. net/) features a collection of more than 1,000 topical guides to various Internet information resources created by librarians and other information professionals. The Clearinghouse reviews and assigns guides an overall rating, based on five criteria, to ensure that it qualifies for acceptance in the Clearinghouse. Criteria include how well the author of the guide describes the contents of the guide and the caliber of resources the author uses, in addition to the guide's design, organizational scheme, and meta-information. The Clearinghouse also strives to point to the most up-to-date guides. *Kathy Schrock's Guide for Educators*, (http://www.capecod.net/schrockguide/) developed by Schrock, a technology coordinator for a Massachusetts School District, is one of the guides listed under the Clearinghouse's Education category. Schrock describes and categorizes the multitude of Internet resources with K-12 educational value, making it easier for educators to locate and identify sites of interest to them—both for their own professional development and to use with their students. Schrock also includes detailed information on search tools.

Public Librarian Jennifer Levine gears her resource guide, *Jenny's Cybrary to the Stars* (http://sashimi.wwa.com/~jayhawk/index.html), to the informational (and entertainment) needs of public librarians. Her page (in addition to including a link to Dilbert) features a Site of the Day ("Always a site with some reference value!") to help librarians stay informed of notable Web sites, and other resources for staying current on the Internet and for discussing Internet access with library board members.

In addition to developing resource guides that serve specific audiences, librarians are coordinating large-scale indexing and cataloging projects to help direct their patrons to valuable Web sites and other Internet resources. Instead of simply providing an alphabet-

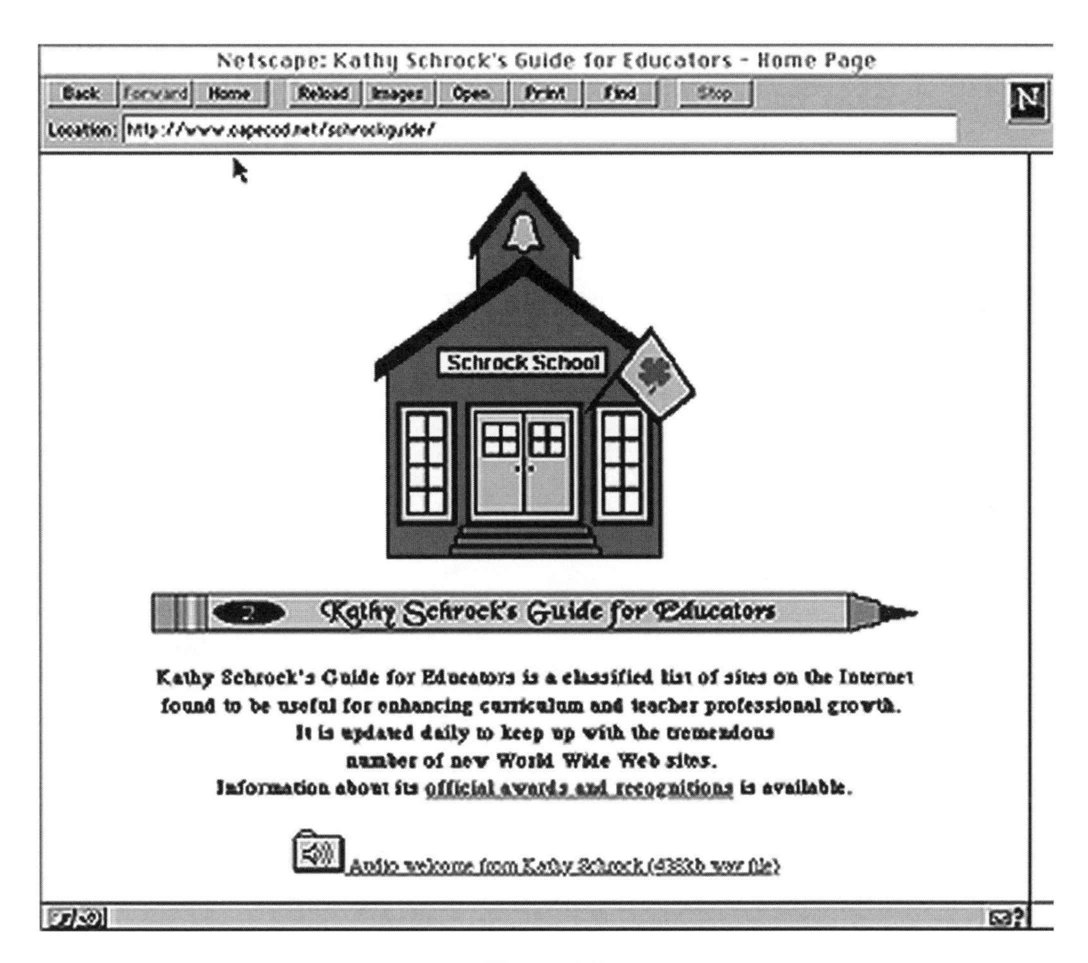

Figure 1.2
An Example of an Internet Resource Guide for Educators

ized list of "cool" or interesting sites, many libraries have begun categorizing Web sites along traditional organizational schemes, such as the Library of Congress or Dewey Decimal classification system. An especially impressive project, *Cyberstacks* (http://www.public.iastate.edu/~CYBERSTACKS/), developed by Gerry McKiernan of Iowa State University, uses Library of Congress call numbers to categorize selected WWW and other Internet resources of a research or scholarly nature. All of *Cyberstacks'* resources include a brief summary and are full-text, hypertext, or hypermedia. From the *Cyberstacks'* home page, McKiernan includes a link to several of his other projects. *Beyond Bookmarks: Schemes for Organizing the Web* (http://www.public.iastate.edu/~CYBERSTACKS/CTW.htm) is one such project which lists some of the different methods libraries have used to facilitate access to Internet resources.

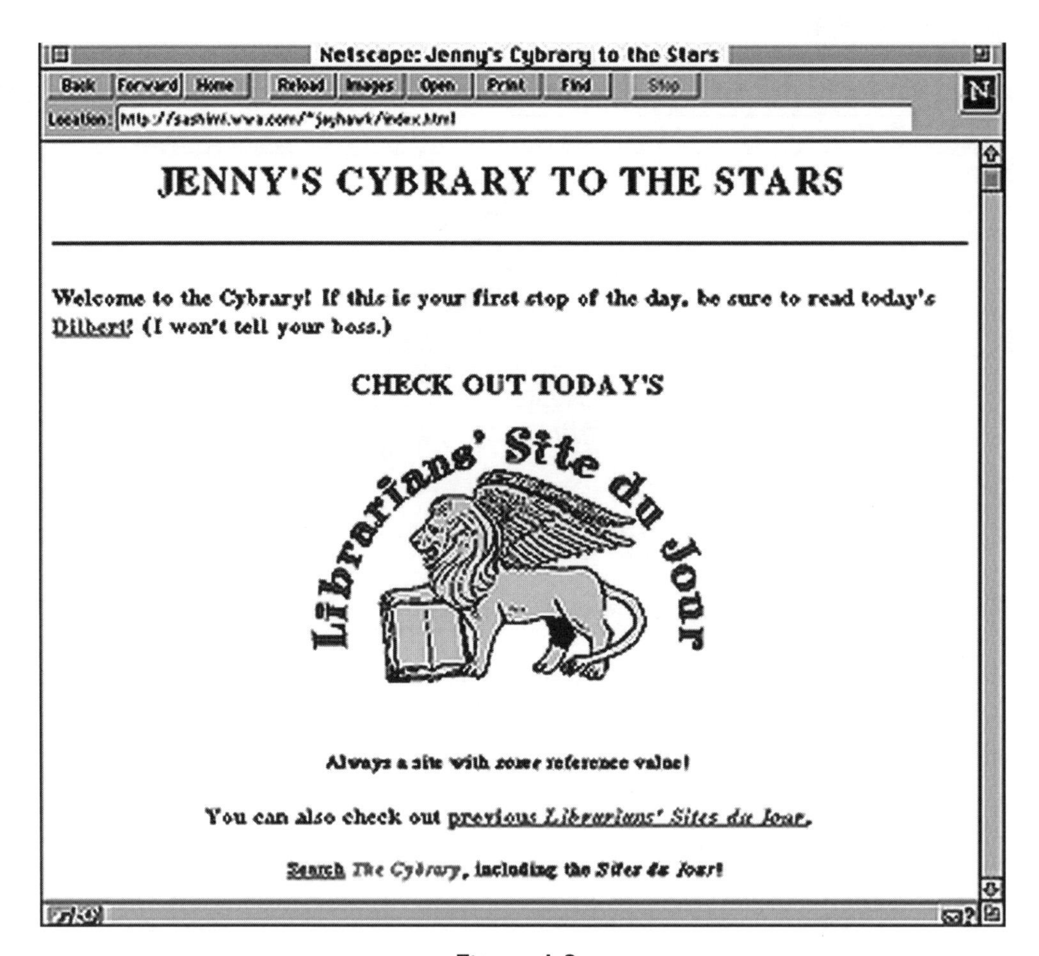

Figure 1.3
Resource Guides Can Be Entertaining as Well as Informative

METHODS FOR ORGANIZING WEB RESOURCES

InfoMINE (http://lib-www.ucr.edu/infomine/exp/), an exemplary academic site from the University of California, Riverside, also uses Library of Congress Subject Headings to help faculty, students, and research staff find and use relevant Web and Internet resources. The creators of the site note:

> Among the contributions of INFOMINE is the essential enrichment or "value added" service, of providing concise descriptive information (an annotation as well as in-depth indexing terminology) for each record. This greatly helps users to quickly retrieve a focused results set, examine the relevance of individual records and then choose among them immediately prior to accessing, thus saving considerable time.

Librarian-developed Web guides serve the same purpose as traditional bibliographies and pathfinders: They help direct patrons through a maze of information by identifying and describing resources with valuable content, reducing the amount of time patrons must sift through layers of information on their own before discovering the source that provides what they really need. Librarians who take the time to select and categorize Web sites into a structure familiar to patrons help to focus their patrons' search for relevant information. (Examples of different kinds of Web resource guides are included on the CD-ROM in the "Designing a Library Web Site" section.)

Library Web sites often replicate two common organizational structures familiar to most public library users: Simple subject headings and the Dewey Decimal system. Many public libraries seem to take a general subject heading approach to organizing guides to Web sites. For example, the Spokane Public Library Subject Index (http://splnet.spokpl.lib.wa.us/subject.html) includes links that are "consistent with Spokane Public Library's mission, operating principles, and service roles as defined in our Collection Development Policy."

Librarian Carole Leita also takes a subject heading approach to her collection of notable Web sites, but the brief annotations she writes for the sites included in BPL's Index to the Internet (which in March, 1997 was renamed the Librarians' Index to the Internet and moved to http://sunsite.berkeley.edu/Internet Index/) are what makes it so valuable and a more useful starting point than the larger but non-descript indexing provided through Yahoo, a popular Internet search index. The BPL Index also is geared to public library users and targets community information, as well. Leita, who adds new sites to the Index weekly says she spends about 4 to 5 hours a week on the project. "It has become my life's work," she says, "but it helps keep me up on the Internet. I think it's important."

Some libraries have attempted to categorize their collections of Web resources according to the Dewey Decimal system, the classification system used by most public libraries in the United States. Morton Grove Public Library identifies its Dewey-classified collection of resources as the *Original Webrary* (http://www.nslsilus.org/mgkhome/orrs/webrary.html) and trademarked the name which has been adopted by other public libraries attempting to do the same thing. The Introduction to the *Webrary* explains to users that: "Sites are added to the Webrary based on their usefulness and the presumed authoritativeness and accuracy of their sources. Just as the Library collects books on all subjects and viewpoints, the presence or absence of a subject or viewpoint in the *Webrary* is in no way a reflection of Library policy."

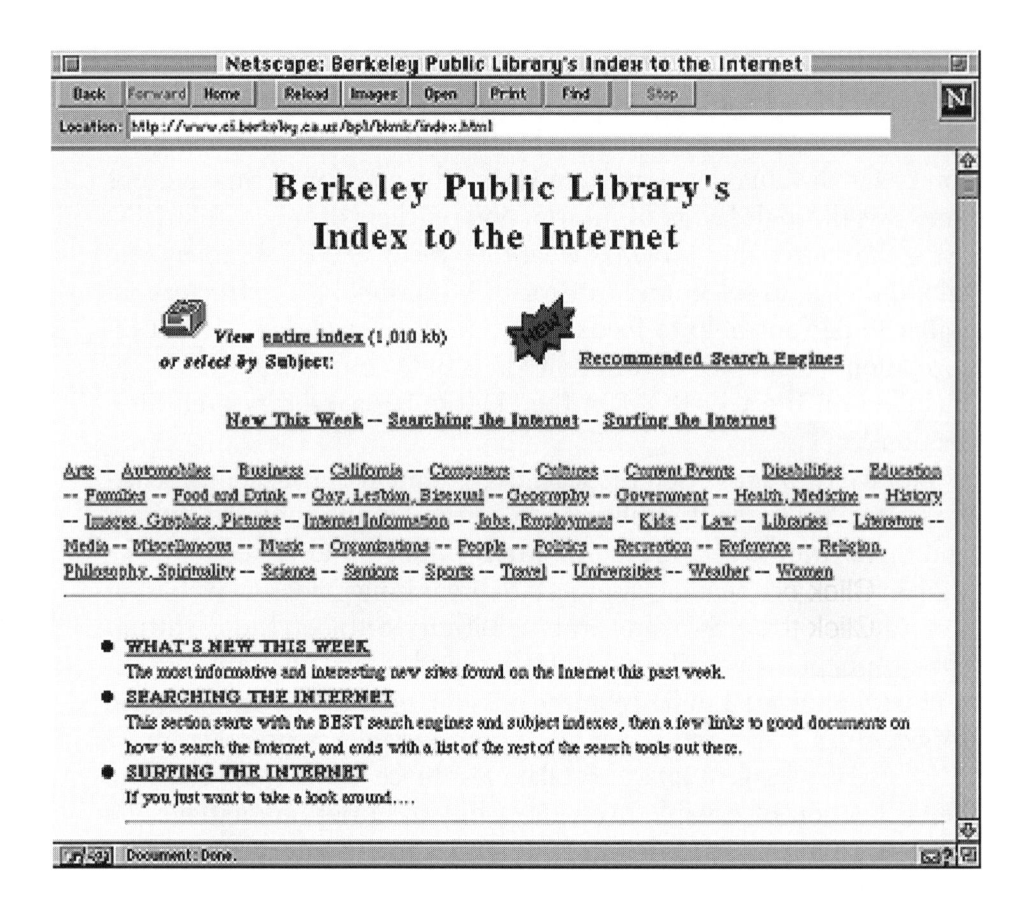

Figure 1.4
The BPL Index has been renamed the Librarians' Index to the Internet and moved to http://sunsite.berkeley.edu/Internet Index

Roberta Johnson, Readers Service Librarian for MGPL who writes most of the annotations for sites included in the *Webrary*, in addition to coordinating her own Virtual Reader's Reference Desk, says it was much more time consuming for the library staff to initially develop the site than it has been to maintain it. "In terms of searching for and evaluating new sites for inclusion in the *Webrary*, we have divided the Dewey hundreds up among our adult services staff. In practice, however, most of our sites are selected by Terry Beck (Reference Coordinator) and Eugenia Bryant (Assistant Director and Head of Public Services)." Johnson estimates that she and Beck spend about an hour a day evaluating new sites and writing annotations.

CyberDewey (http://ivory.lm.com/~mundie/DDHC/CyberDewey.html), developed by programmer David Mundie, offers an even more detailed collection of Web sites organized by Dewey principles. And the Online Computer Library Center (OCLC) is conducting several research projects exploring the indexing and cataloging of electronic resources. Its *Scorpion Project* (http://orc.rsch.oclc.org:6109/) focuses on creating tools that would help automate the process of categorizing Web resources by standard schemes, such as the Dewey System. Such automated procedures will become more and more essential as the Web continues to grow and the demand for accessing and maintaining electronic information escalates, notes Keith Schafer in his introduction to the *Scorpion Project*. Rather than diminish the need for librarians, the development of these automated cataloging tools should entreat librarians to contribute their veritable skills as "order makers" to the management of Internet resources.

To visit the Web sites referenced in this chapter, follow these steps:

1. Open the CD-ROM with your Internet connection running.
2. From the Table of Contents page, click on **Chapter Bibliographies**
3. Click on **Design Guidelines**.
4. Click the link of the site you want to visit.

Chapter 2

Exploring Intellectual Freedom Issues

INTRODUCTION

This chapter describes some of the non-technical and policy-oriented issues that librarians must confront as they begin to grapple with the Web in the library. First, the chapter briefly reviews Federal legislation which attempts to extend regulatory control over the American portion of the Internet, focusing on how this legislation can affect library practice. Second, there is a discussion of censorship issues that arise as libraries establish their Web presence and of two types of resolutions to censorship problems: filtering software and content rating systems. Third, there is an exploration of a range of broader intellectual freedom issues that are raised when librarians put their libraries on the Internet, including free speech, access, privacy, copyright issues, and the protection of intellectual property. The main lesson that emerges from a consideration of these issues is that librarians must think carefully about what they are doing when they make their organizations part of the global Internet and take advantage of this window of opportunity to develop policies and procedures that will help them manage their corner of the Net. Putting time into policy and procedures development in advance of opening their digital doors will help librarians avoid many sticky problems that quickly arise when they join the Web.

Despite the fact that the "official," high-profile work on digital libraries, some of which is heavily funded by the National Science Foundation, is taking place in major research institutions around the

United States, there is equally important work occurring just outside of the spotlight. Librarians and information professionals are working in the trenches of the digital revolution, beginning the grassroots implementation of the "public" digital library. This is in keeping with the role that the Federal government has described for libraries in the National Information Infrastructure:

> Libraries complement both research and education. They figured first into the NREN and now into the vision of an integrated, broadly useful NII. The High Performance Computing Act of 1991 (PL 102-194) envisioned libraries as both access points for users to utilize the network as well as providers of information resources via the Internet. The [Clinton] administration's characterization of the NII carries forward this expectation, expanding it to include a training function.

Hundreds of efforts are under way in libraries across the United States, ranging from the creation of a library home page listing the hours the library is open, to an e-mail reference service, to the planning and implementation of community-based networking. Librarians and information professionals are in the midst of attempts to provide to their patrons what will certainly become important components of public digital libraries. Their work is typically underfunded and done "on-the-fly," yet they have the potential to generate some of the most innovative educational uses of the evolving national electronic networked environment for meeting the needs of the widest range of individuals.

These librarians are working typically without a blueprint, under time and economic constraints and, with a few exceptions, little assistance from the research community. Their efforts do not come without their attendant risks, and it is extremely important that public and school librarians who are becoming network service, resource, and content providers clearly understand what is involved in their participation in the digital revolution from an issues- and policy-oriented perspective.

REGULATING THE INTERNET: FEDERAL AND STATE LEGISLATION

For most of its short life, the Internet has been the private reserve of scientists, researchers, educators, and college students. In the last five years, through a combination of changes in technology and savvy entrepreneurship, the Internet has become the communications medium of the masses. Millions of "newbies" have begun exploring the "information superhighway" and have come onto the Net as commercial Internet service providers have convinced them that acquiring an Internet account is similar to hooking up to a cable television company. Professors Hoffman, Kalsbeek, and Novak "estimate that 28.8 million people in the United States 16 and over have potential or actual access to the Internet, 16.4 million people use the Internet, [and] 11.5 million people use the Web."

Add to this estimate the fact that the size of the Web is doubling every five months, and the increasing prominence of the Net in the media and popular culture is not at all surprising. Now that the "rest of the world" has begun to roam the Net and there are real dollars at stake, the private sector has jumped in and has begun to search for ways to make profit from these new users. Following hot on the heels of the digital entrepreneurs have been politicians, spurred by protests from such diverse interest groups as the telecommunications industry and conservative watchdog groups. This has led to ongoing attempts in the United States throughout this decade to impose some type of regulatory control on the digital content that streams ceaselessly across the Internet. The question is no longer whether librarians should pay attention to these efforts, but how they should react should some form of regulatory control be enacted into law, upheld by the courts, and enforced.

Many previous attempts to impose a regulatory regime on the Internet did not survive challenges within Congress, but, on February 8, 1996, President Clinton signed into law *The Telecommunications Act of 1996*. This law is a major revision of the 1934 Communications Act, which has provided the legislative basis for the growth and development of telecommunications in the United States for more than 60 years. It is also the first Federal law explicitly concerned with control of the Internet. The Act has some sections that would seem to be beneficial, for example, the call for the provision of universal access; according to a White House press release, the Administration wants to do the following:

> Ensure that all Americans have access to the benefits of the information superhighway. The Act ensures that schools, libraries, hospitals and clinics have access to advanced telecommunications services, and calls for them to be connected to the information superhighway by the year 2000. It will help connect every school child in every classroom in America to the information superhighway—opening up worlds of knowledge and opportunities in rural and low-income areas.

Within hours, however, the American Civil Liberties Union, along with many other organizations, filed a lawsuit in District Court in

Philadelphia challenging Title V, Section 502: "Obscene or Harassing Use of Telecommunications Facilities under the Communications Act of 1934," also known as the Communications Decency Act (CDA). (*Note*: For more information, see Appendix A, "Text of the Communications Decency Act.") Although the outcome of the legal challenges to the CDA is uncertain at the time of this writing, it is important to consider its provisions, because they will, in all likelihood, reappear in subsequent legislation in modified form should the original Act be struck down. What was it about this section of the law that caused such a rapid and virulent reaction?

Sections 501 and 502 of the Act clearly set out the boundaries of acceptable behavior on the Internet, and the point seems to be to provide protection for Internet users under the age of 18. According to these provisions of the Act, a person is legally liable if he or she uses an "interactive computer service" to send to or cause to be displayed to a young person "any comment, request, suggestion, proposal, image, or other communication" that meets these criteria:

- That, in context, depicts or describes, in terms patently offensive as measured by contemporary community standards, sexual or excretory activities or organs, regardless of whether the user of such service placed the call or initiated the communication; or
- Which is obscene, lewd, lascivious, filthy, or indecent, with intent to annoy, abuse, threaten, or harass another person; or
- Which is obscene or indecent, knowing that the recipient of the communication is under 18 years of age, regardless of whether the maker of such communication placed the call or initiated the communication.

According to the plaintiffs and many other commentators, the Act is unconstitutional because it criminalizes speech that is ordinarily protected by the First Amendment if the speech can be accessed by people under the age of 18. The wording of the Act is such that providers of the interactive computer communication systems are held to be as culpable as the users of the systems in the event that the law is violated. The plaintiffs also assert that the Act is unconstitutional because it is also impermissibly overbroad and vague; they also point out that it is not the least restrictive means of accomplishing any compelling governmental purpose, which is ordinarily a criterion for enacting legislation restricting activities. Although there is little dispute over the legal meaning of "obscenity," terms such as "lewd, lascivious, and filthy" do not have clear legal meaning, and indecent speech among adults has a tradition of being constitutionally protected.

They also argue that the Act requires that the content of the Internet be reduced to the lowest common moral denominator, so that the "effect of this statute, if implemented, would be to reduce adults to obtaining access by computer to only that information that is fit for children." The effect would be that public discussion on electronic networks would be restricted under the claim that it harms children; under this law, some literary classics, including versions of the Bible, and public health information, such as information about sexually transmitted diseases, AIDS, and abortion can no longer be made available on the Internet by content providers in the United States and can no longer be discussed on computer conferences and USENET newsgroups by citizens of the United States.

An example of Internet regulation occurring at the state level is *HB 1630 Computer or telephone network; transmitting misleading data*, which became law in Georgia in April, 1996. In that state, it is now illegal to do the following:

> Transmit any data through a computer network or over the transmission facilities or through the network facilities of a local telephone network for the purpose of setting up, maintaining, operating, or exchanging data with an electronic mailbox, home page, or any other electronic information storage bank or point of access to electronic information if such data uses any individual name, trade name, registered trademark, logo, legal or official seal, or copyrighted symbol to falsely identify the person, organization, or representative transmitting such data or which would falsely state or imply that such person, organization, or representative has permission or is legally authorized to use [these materials].

One interpretation of this law is that it is now (as of the writing of this book) illegal in Georgia for a person to have an Internet UserID or e-mail address that uses anything other than the person's legal name, because to do otherwise would "falsely identify the person" on a computer network. It certainly violates this law for a person to post an e-mail message to a computer conference using a *nom de plume*, a right that is legally protected in print media. It also now is illegal in Georgia to create a link from a Web page located in Georgia to any other Web page without the explicit permission or legal authorization from the owner of the page to which the link would be established.

There are serious implications for librarians and information professionals if these laws survive their court challenges. Even if these laws do not stand, federal and state legislators will surely be introducing revised versions that attempt to cover the same regulatory ground. Public and school librarians who manage Internet connections in their organizations will have to pay attention to the legislative and judicial events which define these regulatory efforts. Given the two laws mentioned above, it is clear that, at the very least, librarians will have to be very careful about the content they provide, the sites they design and mount on the Web, and the ways in which their systems are used by patrons. It is possible that they and other providers of Internet content would be required to verify the identities and ages of all recipients of material that might be deemed inappropriate for children, making necessary the creation of digital circulation records for their users and ratings evaluations for tens of thousands of Internet sites. They will find themselves in the uncomfortable position of having to act as censors and monitors, which will, in all likelihood, place them in direct opposition to their professional code of ethics.

RATING SYSTEMS AND FILTERING SOFTWARE

Two related strategies that librarians can consider to cope with these regulatory regimes involve ratings systems and Internet filtering or blocking software. These strategies are being proposed by researchers and commercial vendors in an effort to convince politicians that "the Net can take care of itself." The proponents of these efforts hope that they will, if successful, convince would-be regulators that, like the movie or television industries, a self-imposed rating is better than legislated control of the Internet.

One interesting example of a rating system has been proposed by the World Wide Web (W3) Consortium that is being designed to take advantage of filtering or blocking software without being tied to any one product. *The Platform for Internet Content Selection* (PICS) "facilitates the development of technologies to let parents and teachers control what children access on the Internet." The creators of this scheme are attempting to define an open standard for labels that can be used to rate Internet content and will have applicability at three levels; labels can be produced and implemented by the content provider, the service or access provider, and/or the parent. Once in place, the PICS label will be able to be recognized and processed by a wide range of blocking and filtering software. Resnick and Miller describe this as "flexible blocking":

> PICS separates the selection software from the rating labels: any PICS-compliant selection software can read any PICS-compliant labels. In fact, a single site or document may have many la-

> bels, provided by different organizations. Consumers choose their selection software and label sources.
>
> The separation of selection software from rating services will enable both markets to flourish. Software companies and online services that prefer to remain value-neutral can offer selection software without providing any rating labels; values-oriented organizations can offer labels, even if they lack the expertise to write selection software.

A range of filtering and blocking software is currently available. Although the marketing information of each product emphasizes its differences, they all serve a similar function for users: restricting access to sites on the Internet, including Web sites, chat rooms, and USENET newsgroups, and preventing the downloading of certain types of files, such as images (in formats including .jpg, and .gif) and multimedia (in formats .mpg, .avi, and more). These products are written for a variety of platforms, and most will be available for Web servers, Macintosh and PC computers. We will not discuss these products by name; however, interested readers can use their favorite World Wide Web search tool (search for *filtering blocking software*) to locate the home pages of many of the blocking and filtering software vendors. Many software manufacturers offer demonstration versions of their products for downloading and evaluation.

One important way in which these products differentiate themselves is in their blocking procedures. Some contain a predetermined database of sites deemed inappropriate by the vendors; these will have to be continually updated as the Web continues to grow, involving free or for-fee updating. This type of product looks for marketing advantage by emphasizing the size of its database or dictionary (one product boasts a database of over 7,500 objectionable sites) and ease and frequency of updating. Some vendors even have begun to solicit the URLs of objectionable sites from visitors to their Web sites! Other products allow the user to configure the software adding to and deleting sites from the database. These products are beginning to offer features that track all Internet activity on the computer, allow the user to configure the software to prevent the use of certain credit cards for Internet commerce from that computer, and block access based on the discovery of restricted words and phrases used in context. Many are now announcing that they are "PICS" compliant.

Rating systems and blocking and filtering software offer parents, educators, and librarians a range of options for restricting users' access to certain areas in cyberspace that are inappropriate or objectionable. As more vendors adopt standard systems such as PICS and their products become more sophisticated, the appeal of this strategy increases. Public and school librarians, however, should think carefully about the extent to which they wish to become involved in restricting patron access to the Internet. By using software with a predetermined set of blocked sites, they are acquiescing to the standards of the vendor without a clear understanding of the fit between those standards and the selection principles they have implemented in their non-networked collection development policies. By using a rating system which contains labels that they did not create, they are allowing others outside of their libraries to create *de facto* standards of acceptability that they will use. Unlike the rating systems used by the entertainment industry, which are based on standards set by a central body and used by all parties, rating systems for Internet content are, at the moment, decentralized, and are based on widely varying definitions of acceptability. This should give librarians pause.

BROADER INTELLECTUAL FREEDOM CONSIDERATIONS

Assuming that librarians can come to reasonable decisions about the use of ratings and filtering software, there is still a range of issues and concerns that must be considered by those who are building and managing public digital libraries; these will vary with the setting within which the development effort takes place. Public and school libraries operate under varying institutional constraints and it is reasonable to expect that librarians exploring the possibilities of establishing a Net presence for their libraries will have access to different resources and will face different problems in their work.

There is a presentation on the CD-ROM that provides more background information about the range of intellectual freedom issues that can arise when public and school libraries offer Internet access. To access the presentation, follow these steps:

1. Open the CD-ROM and display the Table of Contents.
2. Click on **Intellectual Freedom**. The Intellectual Freedom and the Library page appears.
3. Click **presentation** in the first paragraph to get started.

The complexity of the technical challenges that must be faced and overcome in these settings is neither trivial nor easily managed. However, an equally challenging set of issues organized around the concept of intellectual freedom also must be faced and managed. These are issues that have been recognized as being central to librarianship; however, in the electronic networked information environment they have not been given sufficient attention. The purpose here is to bring these issues to the foreground in an attempt to spur practitioners into thinking about them; there will not be an attempt to resolve them here, for these issues will vary widely with the setting and have a tendency to shade off quickly into intricate legal discussions. Rather, by explicitly bringing them into view, practitioners can begin to wrestle with them, moving toward a well-thought out and defensible acceptable use policy that protects the library without infringing on the rights of users. This is in keeping with the American Library Association, which takes the position that:

> Issues arising from the still-developing technology of computer-mediated information generation, distribution, and retrieval need to be approached and regularly reviewed from a context of constitutional principles and established policy, so that fundamental and traditional tenets of librarianship are not swept away.

In each of the following sections, a brief scenario is used to focus the discussion of the issues; these scenarios are descriptive and are intended to provoke reflection. This will be followed by questions intended to sharpen the issue and excerpts from the American Library Association's recently adopted resolution about patron access to electronic information, services, and networks, which stakes out the broad guidelines for the profession.

Free Speech

> *A patron brings a disk in to the library, uploads a document that contains hateful material denigrating particular ethnic groups and advocating racial separation, and sends it as e-mail to many computer conferences and USENET newsgroups, and some selected individuals. Each time the message arrives at its destination, it carries header information identifying it as having come from the library.*

Can the library deny the patron's right to broadcast the document? What are the limits of a patron's constitutionally protected speech when using the public or school library's Internet connection to engage in communication with others (privately and in computer conferences)? According to attorneys Cavazos and Morin, "the right to speak one's mind without fear of government retribution is perhaps the most cherished of all the rights guaranteed by the U.S. Constitution." What should be the position of the library on the issue of the protection of the patron's right to freedom of expression, which includes both the freedom of speech and the right to receive information?

More specifically, the question concerns the extent to which the rights of the patron using the library's Internet access to participate in public and private electronic communications must be balanced against the responsibilities of the library as the provider of the resources and services. Are there or should there be any restrictions on a patron's ability to use an e-mail account or other Internet resources provided by the library to send or receive any type of electronic message to another person, organization, or computer conference? This situation is exacerbated by the fact that many libraries are experimenting with WWW access, using browsers such as Netscape, Mosaic, or Internet Explorer, all of which allow the user to send e-mail without closing the browser and with varying degrees of anonymity. (*Note:* It is possible to disable the mailer on most WWW browsers, effectively preventing user from being able to invoke the mailing and newsgroup posting functions, but this is a neither trivial nor obvious procedure. There are also procedures that can be invoked such as the use of password protection to restrict users' access to certain browser features.)

The ALA recently clarified its position on the issue of free speech by asserting that "Users should not be restricted or denied access for expressing or receiving constitutionally protected speech." This would seem to indicate that, in the above scenario, the patron should be allowed to carry on, so long as his speech does not become obscene or harassing. This raises the dilemma of achieving a reasonable balance between editorial control and tolerance in official policy statements of user rights, responsibilities, and acceptable use. If a given computer conference and other sites where the patron engages in the potentially hateful communication can be defined as a "limited public forum," then the case for restricting speech is weakened, because "the owner of that particular forum no longer has the right to control and censor speech activities there." This matter is further complicated by the realization that the issue of the ownership of the Internet is far from clear.

The protection of patrons' rights to express themselves freely using the Internet facilities in their public library is also supported by the National Research Council, albeit for different reasons:

> Providers that assert the right to control the content of public traffic may be subject to a more stringent liability (e.g., for defamation) for that traffic than those that do not assert such a right . . . Information services supported by public funds, operated by government, or otherwise deemed public cannot discriminate among users on the basis of their electronic communications for First Amendment reasons . . . Service providers of all types are well advised to establish the rules under which they provide their services, preferably in advance and perhaps in consultation with their users.

Public and school librarians would do well to heed this advice and have a set of clearly established policies for handling situations where patrons use the library's Internet connection to engage in the type of communication that skirts the borders of constitutionally protected speech.

Privacy

> *Your library has been running its Web site for several months and you sit down to talk with the systems librarian, who has become the library's "Webmistress." You ask how many people have been visiting the site and how many have used the electronic reference service that can be accessed from the library's home page. To your surprise, she tells you the exact number of people, where they went, how long they stayed, what their userIDs are, and the names of the machines they used to access the site. She also tells you that there is a complete archive of every e-mail and form-based reference question and all of the reference librarian's responses. She asks you what to do with this information.*

If a library operates an Internet Reference desk, as is being done at the Internet Public Library, all incoming reference questions and outgoing responses can be easily captured and stored in a searchable database. If a library has a Web site on its own server, the recording of statistical and other more personal information about visitors to the site is nearly automatic. These features of networking software enable the amassing of detailed statistics that will provide the librarians with a clearer understanding of the efficiency of their reference work, the diversity of questions that arrive as e-mail, the usefulness of their reference collection, and the usability of their Web site. This information, however, also raises privacy concerns, because, in addition to the content of the e-mail messages, the attached header information is also captured. Unlike the face-to-face reference interview, where the question can be logged and time-on-task recorded, electronic, networked reference work allows the capturing of personal information about the sender of the question the confidentiality of which the library must be careful to preserve. There will also be information about specific users and their use of the library's Web pages.

MOO: A Multi-User Object Oriented environment, an interactive system accessible through telnet by many users at the same time.

A similar concern is raised by MOO-based reference work, where users must log on, again providing the host (in this case the library) with personal information. Using a MOO-based reference work, a line-by-line verbatim transcript easily can be saved and stored, each line of which can be matched to the userID of the person who keyed it in. This obviously is a boon to the researcher interested in careful textual analysis of the reference interview interaction, but again, the librarian must be concerned with the preservation of the patron's privacy. A related privacy concern arises in the instance where the library hosts computer conferences through its WWW site, using LISTSERV software or through the creation of a USENET group. The library is then in possession of the database of subscribers, containing their names and e-mail addresses and, if archived, a complete transcript of all of the messages posted to the conference.

One position on the issue of the privacy of this information is that it should receive the same protection as is afforded to circulation information. The ALA seems to agree, arguing that, in the electronic, networked, information environment:

> Users have both the right of confidentiality and the right of privacy. The library should uphold these rights by policy, procedure, and practice. Users should be advised, however, that because security is technically difficult to achieve, electronic transactions and files could become public.

A good example of language in a policy statement intended to deal with the ease with which personal information can be collected about individuals using the public digital library's resources and services is found in the *Server Access Log Policy* of the Internet Public Library:

> No Library records shall be made available to the public, press, or governmental agency, except by such process, order, or subpoena authorized by national, state or local law. The Director of the Library shall resist such process, order, or subpoena until there is a proper show of good cause. Any costs incurred by

the Library in any search of records shall be charged to the agency demanding such a search.

The importance of such language cannot be underemphasized because of the need to protect the confidentiality of the patron's personal information in an environment where it can be easily collected and manipulated in digital form. Librarians should develop an explicit policy statement that ensures patrons that the library extends the same degree of protection to information collected about their Internet use in the library as it does for information about their other library uses.

Access

A patron regularly uses WWW search tools to run searches for sites with sexual themes. He takes delight in downloading and displaying images and multimedia that he finds on Web sites and in USENET newsgroups on the high resolution monitor. He asks at the reference desk for help in printing the images on the library's printer. A milder form of this scenario might be the patron requesting that the library provide access to certain USENET newsgroups in the .alt hierarchy that espouse racial warfare and separation of the races.

Can the library deny this patron access to the Internet connection? Would the situation be different if the patron was searching for politically sensitive information, such as pro- or anti-abortion sites? Are there reasonable grounds for refusing a patron access to the library's Internet services and resources? Should the library consider restricting access to computer conferences such as the infamous ".alt" hierarchy in USENET?

The ALA does not believe that there are *a priori* grounds for denying patrons access to networked information resources and services, arguing that "electronic information, services, and networks provided directly or indirectly by the library should be equally, readily, and equitably accessible to all library users." Further, librarians should not be placed in the position of having to make decisions about the quality of the resources and services that patrons may access and, on the touchy issue of allowing minors access to the full range of the Internet, ALA states forcefully that access restrictions are the provenance of parents:

Providing connections to global information, services, and networks is not the same as selecting and purchasing material for a library collection. Determining the accuracy or authenticity of electronic information may present special problems. Some information accessed electronically may not meet a library's selection or collection development policy. It is, therefore, left to each user to determine what is appropriate. Parents and legal guardians who are concerned about their children's use of electronic resources should provide guidance to their own children.

Libraries and librarians should not deny or limit access to information available via electronic resources because of its allegedly controversial content or because of the librarian's personal beliefs or fear of confrontation. Information retrieved or utilized electronically should be considered constitutionally protected unless determined otherwise by a court with appropriate jurisdiction.

Perhaps questions of access can be handled by education; librarians may wish to consider developing programming to educate their patrons about the complexities, rights, and responsibilities of Internet use, following the observation of the United States National Information Infrastructure Advisory Council that "schools, libraries, and community centers have an interest in encouraging their constituents to use information in lawful and ethical ways."

Intellectual Property

You've decided to take the plunge and develop your own Web site. The person you've placed in charge reports back to you and is proud of her work. She points out that the HTML markup was simplified because she was able to access other pages and easily cut and paste their markup into the library's pages, including a "guestbook." She is also excited by her ability to easily download images and icons she finds on other Web pages and place them onto the library's pages.

Guestbook: A database of information about people created when they submit information in a form on a Web page.

The trend seems to be for public and school libraries to establish their Internet presences on the WWW, especially since the primary markup language (Hypertext Markup Language or HTML) has proven to be fairly easy to learn and use. In the scenario described above, the question is whether the various elements that constitute a WWW page are fair game simply because most browsers allow users to access the markup code for any page on the Web? Is there any problem in copying and using images and "scripts" from other people's sites? It is clear that current networking hardware and software make the copying and transfer of digital information simple and relatively painless, especially when using WWW browsers. It is much less clear what type of copying and use of what can be found on the WWW is legitimate and what constitutes a violation of copyright.

Current copyright legislation protects the original expression of a fact or idea or of compilations of facts or ideas as soon as the work is fixed in a tangible medium. In fact,

> Any work created while using the information superhighway is automatically protected by Federal copyright law as soon as it is fixed in the computer's memory. The creator does not need to apply for a copyright, register the creation with a government office, or even place a notice of copyright on it. The result is that she can, if she chooses to do so, prevent others from making various unauthorized uses of the new material.

Current legislation also establishes the conditions under which use of the copyrighted material is legitimate. When, then, can the downloading and use of the images, arrangement of HTML tags, and CGI or Java scripts of another Web page be considered fair use? This is perhaps the murkiest of the issues that have been raised thus far. Currently, experts in intellectual property and copyright law are just beginning to grapple with these issues. At the moment it is a gray area, so librarians would be well advised to seek permission for the use of digital imagery and scripts unless they are explicitly labeled as being either freeware or in the public domain.

Another interesting problem is raised by the ease with which one WWW page can be linked to another page using HTML tags; this is at least partially responsible for the phenomenal growth of the WWW, but it can raise a problem for a library if the library's Webmistress finds that the library's page has been linked to a page that seems to be offensive or objectionable. It is also important to note that linking is mostly a one-way phenomenon; if I link to your site, you are under no obligation to link to my site. At present, there is no protocol beyond HTML which determines the procedures by which two sites can be linked and nothing more binding than common courtesy determining the appropriateness of the resulting links. In a sense, the owner of a Web page cannot prevent another from making use of the page through linking and cannot prevent the subsequent display of her or his intellectual property. The designer or owner of a public digital library site has little more than his or her powers of persuasion in the event that his or her page has been linked to a site that, by the standards and policies of the library, is deemed unacceptable.

CONCLUSIONS

Clearly, there is a strong emphasis on the extension of digital libraries into public and school libraries in some as-of-yet undetermined form. According to the NTIA Office of Telecommunications and Information Applications:

> Connecting every classroom, library, hospital, and clinic in the United States to the National Information Infrastructure (NII) is a priority for the Clinton Administration. It is critical for these public institutions to become and remain active participants in the NII, since they can use telecommunications and information technologies to benefit all Americans.

Putting aside for a moment the technical and economic issues involved in creating and maintaining a digital library in a public or school library setting, it is clear that there are layers of complexity involved in applying the principles of intellectual freedom to public digital library service. As stated by J.F. Krug, Director of the American Library's Office of Intellectual Freedom, in the *Intellectual Freedom Manual,* 5th Edition, there is a set of issues that must be separated and carefully studied by librarians and information professionals so that they can clarify the policies that are necessary to ensure, to the fullest extent, that they and their patrons "can escape the whims of the censor and enjoy the full benefit of freedom of expression under the First Amendment."

These issues include the preservation of free speech when communicating on the global Internet, the right of the patron to privacy, particularly in the realm of personal information in electronic form, the provision of access to electronic, networked resources and services in the public or school library, and the protection of digital intellectual property. Examples of acceptable use policies created by public and school libraries that attempt to come to grips with these issues have been gathered by Web authors Champelli and Ingram, and a sympathetic critique of this type of policy is offered by Kinneman, an analyst, author, and lecturer on Internet topics. These are not trivial matters to resolve; librarians and information professionals must begin a critical public discussion towards two complementary ends: the clarification of the range of positions that be taken in the profession on these issues and the development of practical and workable policies that can provide assistance and support to those in the trenches of the digital revolution.

Chapter 3

Developing Internet Acceptable Use Policies

INTRODUCTION

Librarians are practiced policymakers. They have policies on hand for the selection, circulation, and deselection of materials, as well as for how to respond when library materials are challenged. Policies for programming, public use of library meetings rooms, exhibit spaces, and the confidentiality of library records also are common. But why would a library need an Acceptable Use Policy? Until recently, this was an unfamiliar term. As more and more libraries have started providing Internet access to the public, however, Acceptable Use Policies (AUPs) have taken a prominent position in library policy manuals and on library Web pages. (*Note:* Some libraries name these policies differently; for example, your library may use the phrase *Internet Use Policy* or *Internet Access Policy*.)

Why has the AUP become an essential document for the provision of Internet access? Does a library really need one? This chapter aims to answer these questions in the course of reviewing what an AUP is and defining its relationship to other policies and professional guidelines advanced by the American Library Association. This chapter also explores how academic, school and public libraries have attempted to integrate AUPs with existing policies and balance the competing interests they often embody.

WHAT IS AN AUP?

Acceptable Use Policies (AUPs) dictate the types of activities that may be performed and the kinds of information and communications that may be transmitted on any specific computer network, whether it's a local area network or the global connection of computers known as the Internet. As attorney Lance Rose explains: "At the core of nearly every relationship between online system and user lies a contract. The user contract is a tool for making every online system a productive, stable environment. By spelling out the rules in advance, system operators and users each know what is expected of them." Although not all library policies for Internet access can be considered "contracts," and names for these documents vary from *Computer Use Policy* to *Policy for Access to Networked Information Resources*, they are commonly referred to as *Internet Acceptable Use Policies*.

Internet Acceptable Use Policy seems to be a contradiction of terms—the controlling function of an AUP conflicts with the unregulatable nature of the Internet and culture of self-governance perpetuated by its users. Nevertheless, the term has stuck. Use of the term in the networked environment originated with the National Science Foundation's development of the United States' Internet backbone, NSFnet, designed to promote the free exchange of scholarly communication among academic, government, and other institutional researchers. To ensure that NSFnet would be used to foster education and research—and not corporate profit-making—the NSF's Acceptable Use Policy prohibited use of the world's largest networked information system for commercial purposes or for extensive private or personal business.

Regional Internet providers, organizations that connect community networks to the NSFnet backbone, have their own acceptable use policies, many of which permit product advertisements and other commercial activities. For example, the *Acceptable Use Policy* for SURAnet, a regional network sponsored by the Southeastern Universities Research Association, states "SURAnet traffic need not conform to the NSFnet Acceptable Use Agreement and there is no prohibition on commercial traffic."

The influx of businesses eager to capitalize on the increasing popularity of the Information Superhighway to the Internet coincided with the NSF's withdrawal of financial support for the U.S. primary Internet backbone, which in the late 1980s became known as the National Information Infrastructure. Many LISTSERVs and newsgroups still discourage commercial announcements and solicitations, but it is common today to see commercial advertisements pop up on Web pages. They appear at the top of pages providing access to search engines, and at the bottom of both commercial and non-profit sites. As a means of supporting Internet services, and particularly the production of Web pages, commercial advertising is no longer taboo.

Acceptance of commercial infiltration hasn't eliminated the need for Internet acceptable use policies, however. On the contrary; as Internet activity has grown, so have the concerns for "acceptable use." Apple Computer's Steve Cisler notes that the arrival of new users to the Internet in the 1990s prompted "a series of cultural and policy-based brush fires" as Internet providers, administrators, and users debated such polarities as anarchic versus governed, private and anonymous versus centralized secure systems with accountability, indexed information versus raw data, unimpeded rivers of data versus filtered, bottled, and marketed information, free speech versus censorship, access for some versus universal access . . . and centralized sources of information versus every user as publisher."

Some of these issues, particularly unrestricted access to information versus filtering what users can access, top the list of concerns for libraries providing public Internet access. The best library Internet AUPs address these and other intellectual freedom issues. As the ALA notes in *Access to Electronic Information, Services, and Networks: an Interpretation of the LIBRARY BILL OF RIGHTS*:

> Issues arising from the still-developing technology of computer-mediated information generation, distribution, and retrieval need to be approached and regularly reviewed from a context of constitutional principles and ALA policies so that fundamental and traditional tenets of librarianship are not swept away.

The Morton Grove Public Library (MGPL) in Illinois is one of many libraries which have put this position into practice by stating in its *Internet Access Policy* that "Access to the Internet is compatible with the Library's endorsement of the *Library Bill of Rights*, the *Freedom to Read*, and the *Freedom to View* statements from the American Library Association and with the Morton Grove Public Library's *Collection Development & Materials Selection Policy* and the Library's *Mission Statement*." Available on the Web, MGPL includes links to all the policies mentioned so that users may read the related documents for themselves.

Libraries that support ALA policies and principles may also want to refer to the ALA's statement on *Access to Electronic Information* in their Internet AUPs. Adopted at ALA's Annual Convention in January 1996, this newest interpretation of the *Library Bill of Rights* directly addresses issues endemic to the provision of Internet access and serves as a useful guideline for the topics that a library's AUP should cover. Notably, the interpretation emphasizes the rights of users of electronic resources, often neglected in AUPs focused on preserving the security of an electronic network. The AUPs discussed in the rest of this chapter will be considered in light of the advice offered by this statement.

To view ALA's statement on *Access to Electronic Information*, follow these steps:

1. Open the CD-ROM and go to the Table of Contents page.
2. Click on **Acceptable Use Policies**.
3. Scroll down to the selection **ALA's Access to Electronic Information, Services and Networks Policy** and click it.

WHY IS AN AUP IMPORTANT FOR LIBRARIES?

There are two main reasons why a library should want to have an Internet AUP: to inform patrons about access to the Internet and to protect itself from potential problems. For people just beginning to comprehend what the Internet is and the kinds of information that are accessible through the WWW, a library's AUP can serve as a teaching tool, giving a brief definition of the Internet, explaining why the library has chosen to invest in making the Internet available to its patrons, describing Internet resources that are available to patrons, and listing any expectations the library has for patrons accessing Internet resources through the library's connection.

The AUP also stands as a measure of defense. Although it serves to educate the public about the Internet and the diversity of materials it makes available, some of which may be offensive, it also helps deflect complaints. Through the AUP, the library can explain that it has no way of controlling or regulating information on the Internet and cannot be held liable for what patrons may encounter during their Internet searches. An effective AUP instructs and guides library staff members' responses to problems that may arise.

Anne Rau, reference librarian at the Clarence H. Rosa Public Library in Lansing, Michigan, describes the dual functions of an AUP when she notes:

> We wrote an Internet policy (as an amendment to our regular collection development policy) in case we get challenges from patrons regarding the controversial items on the Internet. We

> wanted to make it clear that we do not censor the Internet just as we don't censor other library materials, and that parents/guardians of minors are responsible for what minors access, not the library staff.

Could a library simply adopt ALA's Access to Electronic Information statement as its policy on providing public access to the Internet? Certainly this would be better than nothing, as it would at least alert patrons to the library's position on this matter—if the library made an effort to inform patrons of its endorsement of the ALA policy. But libraries serve their patrons best when they apply broad principles of librarianship to their own specific practices. Plus, many library Internet AUPs consist of a general policy, as well as more specific statements on procedures for implementing the policy. Although the ALA's position on *Access to Electronic Information* may recommend policy for libraries, a library's own AUP also explains why and how it proposes to implement that policy.

IS EVERY LIBRARY AUP THE SAME?

"In making decisions about how to offer access to electronic information," the ALA advises, "each library should consider its mission, goals, objectives, cooperative agreements, and the needs of the entire community it serves." Policy analyst Robert Burger also encourages policy makers to consider their goals when creating policy: "Clarity in both the definition of policy goals and policy directions is essential in order to implement a policy. Without goals and specific directions, the implemented policy may not at all resemble the original intent of the policy makers."

The goals, or intent, of policies for public access to the Internet vary according to the kind of library (school, public, or university) providing the access. In some cases, it is not the library or librarians who will establish the terms of an Acceptable Use Policy, but other agencies involved in the provision of access, such as the university computing center, district technology director, or school or library board members. Despite the variations found in AUPs of different institutions, some common goals are apparent: to educate the user about the Internet, to define a person's eligibility for using the computer systems to access the Internet, and to outline the conditions of acceptable use.

Generally, AUPs aim to define and balance the rights and responsibilities of the users with the rights and responsibilities of the providers in an effort to provide unrestricted, equitable access to the Internet. But Cisler warns that as Internet use has expanded and diversified, "many people—including users, administrators, and people not on the Net—are trying to protect people, systems, data from use, abuse, or access." Unfortunately, a concern for "protecting" too often provides a rationale for preventing access. Librarians best serve their community members by making sure the goal of the library's AUP is to provide patrons access to the Internet, not to protect them from it.

Protecting Public Access Computers—Security Measures

In addition to adopting an Acceptable Use Policy, libraries often take additional measures to prevent patrons from tampering with system files, changing the options on the Web browser, or altering other features which are designed for customizing the computer to an individual's use, but which can become security hazards when available in a public computing environment. Methods for securing PCs vary depending on the hardware and software the library uses and network configurations. Because these methods are platform dependent and quickly become highly technical, this book will not discuss PC or network security in detail.

Whatever steps your library takes to protect its public access computers, remember to document what has been done. Make sure that the new automation manager or systems operator can find out what the previous person did to secure PCs. Keep a record of the security software that is being used, if any, and make notes on how you may have edited the Web browser to disable certain options.

The document prepared by the California InFoPeople Project explaining "How to Edit Netscape for Public Access Computer" is available on the CD-ROM. It includes links to several sites off the CD-ROM so it is best to access this resource with your Internet connection running.

1. Open the CD-ROM and display the Table of Contents page.
2. Choose **Acceptable Use Policies**.
3. Click the word **secure** that appears at the end of the first paragraph on the Acceptable Use Policies page. This hyperlink will take you to the bottom of the page where you will find another link to the InFoPeople Project's guidelines for Editing Netscape for Public Access Computers.
4. Near the bottom of the Bibliography for Acceptable Use Policies page on the CD-ROM you'll find links to several Web-based resources that provide more information on security measures you can take to protect public access computers. Here are a few you may want to try:

InfoPeople's Public Access Computer Security
Available at: http://www.lib.berkeley.edu:8000/Security/

Security Issues from OPLIN, the Ohio Public Library Internet Network
Available at: http://www.molo.lib.oh.us/tech/security/default.htm

Public Access Software & Configuration - PC Security Measures/Kiosk Software from Library Land Electronic Resources
Available at: http://www.rcls.org/libland/llelres.htm

Response summary: IKiosk & Fortres for PC security, from Web4Lib Archives
http://www.mccmedia.com:80/Web4Lib/1996/December/13151.html

Search Web4Lib Archives at
http://sunsite.berkeley.edu/Web4Lib/archive.html

Bardon Data Systems, makers of WinU Security Software
Available at: http://www.bardon.com/

Fortres Grand Corporation, makers of Fortres Security Software
Available at: http://www.fortres.com/

Hyper Technologies Inc., makers of IKIOSK Security Software
Available at: http://www.hypertec.com/

The issues are complex, as educators Bill Manning and Don Perkins note in their 1994 *Draft for an Acceptable Use Policy Definition*, because Internet services comprise both information and communication, and because they strive to balance the conflicting needs of users to access information and communication resources with the need for network security. Policies often attempt to maintain this balance by insisting that patrons follow appropriate use guidelines, or lose their access privileges. Other items to consider in the formation of policy, Manning and Perkins advise, include: "privacy, morals and ethics, freedom of expression, legal constraints, safety, harassment, plagiarism, resource utilization, indemnification, targeted areas of interest, expected behaviors, and remedies and recourse."

Legal constraints and *Indemnification* are words that can make even the most stalwart library boards tremble, hedge, and wonder whether providing access to the Internet is something they really want to take on after all. And what role do morals and ethics play? Although libraries strive to provide a values-free forum for diverse viewpoints, a call for moral and ethical use of information networking systems appears regularly in policies addressing acceptable use of the Internet. The second sentence in the ALA's statement on *Access to Electronic Information* asserts that "Based on its constitutional, *ethical*, and historical heritage, American Librarianship is uniquely positioned to address the broad range of information issues being raised in the electronic communications revolution." A portion of the Saint Joseph County (Indiana) Public Library's *Computer Usage Policy* reads: "Computing resources should be used in accordance with the ethical standards of the Library."

With tongue in cheek, Williams College in Massachusetts acknowledges that establishing public policy is a complicated affair, encompassing both legal concerns and societal values. The college titles its Web site listing policies of Williams College's Offices and Departments, not simply *Policies*, but: *Policies, Rules, Laws, Principles, Aphorisms*. In addition to links to the Williams College Computing and Library Policies, the page includes links to United States Law, the *Telecommunications Act of 1996*, the U.S. Constitution, Cybernetic Principles, as well as to a collection of *Aesop's Fables*. The top of the page features a graphic depiction of a "Simple Rule Generation Paradigm."

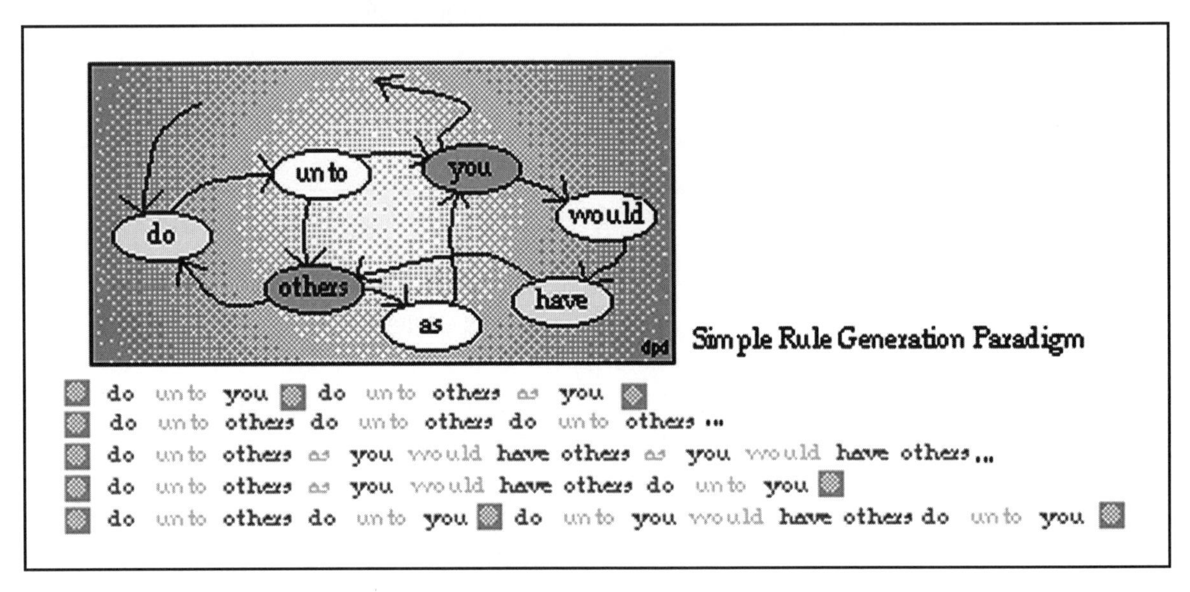

Figure 3.1
Setting Internet Policy Is Challenging, but not Necessarily Humorless

AUPS IN ACADEMIC LIBRARIES

Williams College's philosophical outlook on the challenges of creating public policy that will satisfy everyone may be atypical, but the kinds of policies it offers are not. Because use of the Internet spans multiple computer networks, the rights of the provider as well as the user, communication needs, security requirements, and other issues, a patchwork of policies often are applied to define acceptable use of Internet resources. This is most apparent in academic institutions where use of the Internet generally falls under the college or university's guidelines for using computer resources. Searching for information on Internet acceptable use policies in academic libraries returns pages of policies addressing a myriad of Internet-related activities at colleges and universities. These range from guidelines for creating Web pages to outlines of computer user privileges and responsibilities. Because it's impossible to access the Internet without use of a computer, it makes sense to define acceptable use of the Internet by linking it to appropriate use of university computing resources. Thus, policies for Internet access and use generally are incorporated into the University's guidelines for computer use. Some policies do focus specifically on the Internet, however, and some particularly on the World Wide Web. Florida International University's *World Wide Web Policies* "have been created to define what FIU considers responsible and ethical behavior." The university explains that WWW activities and products must be consistent with its academic ethics, including its *Policy to Prohibit Sexual Harassment* and *Computer Security and Guidelines* as well as with its statement of purpose: "Computer and telecommunications resources have been allocated only for W3 activities that support research, education, administrative processes, FIU sponsored community service and other legitimate pursuits." The policy goes on to list illegitimate pursuits or violations to the stated purpose of telecommunications resources, including "Games not related to FIU programs and/or mission (e.g. Running a simulated baseball league)". The policy concludes by reminding students: "You are the first line of enforcement. Think before you act and understand the consequences of your actions."

As part of its policies for use of computer and information systems, Yale includes an *Institutional WWW Account Information & Policy* for Yale-affiliated organizations seeking space on the institutional Web server. The policy explains that the space may only be used to house "WWW-based documents by approved University organizations and departments" and is not to be used for personal WWW pages, sending e-mail, or any other Internet-related activity. It also directs account holders to construct their Web pages off-line.

In addition to being used ethically and legally in accordance with state and federal telecommunications laws, university computing policies often state that networked facilities are intended for teaching and research purposes and must be used in support of the University's educational mission. Some university libraries support this directive by discouraging or actively prohibiting patrons from using Web browsers to telnet to personal e-mail accounts. When the University of Houston Libraries started providing Web access in January 1995, the library posted a policy stating that its networked workstations were primarily for the use of patrons doing library-related research and that people not doing this type of work may be asked to turn over their workstations to patrons who need them for research. However, in accord with principles of librarianship that seek to preserve the privacy of patrons using library resources and refrain from judging the value or utility of a patron's use of those resources, UH Librarians do not "police" the terminals looking for patrons who violate the policy. Nancy Buchanan, coordinator of electronic resources and chair of the UH Libraries Gopher/Web Task Force, which oversees the development and maintenance of its Web, explains:

> When our networked terminals are full, and patrons are waiting to get on, we make a general announcement that users are waiting, and would those who are using e-mail or chat please finish (with a reminder that they can do this at the main campus computing lab) so others can use the terminals. We do not monitor what users are doing and then select or target individuals and ask specific individuals to get off.

Obviously, the rules an academic library establishes for using Internet resources are closely connected to the number and arrangement of its computer facilities, which tend to be governed by policies set by university computing systems. When the use of new resources, such as the WWW, are not adequately addressed by existing computer use policies, many universities have developed new guidelines. Emory University in Georgia graciously acknowledges the variety of policies from schools around the country that contributed to the development of its new Information Technology Policy, and lightheartedly adds: "We have not succeeded in answering all your questions. The answers we have found only serve to raise a whole set of new questions. In some ways we feel we are as confused as ever, but we believe we are confused on a higher level and about more important things."

To view examples of Acceptable Use Policies from academic institutions, follow these steps:

1. Open the CD-ROM and go to the Table of Contents page.
2. Click on **Acceptable Use Policies**.
3. Scroll down to the "Academic Policies" section and click the name of the example you want to view.

Although appropriate use of the Web and other Internet resources is of concern to academic institutions, academic libraries have not had as urgent a need as public and school libraries to develop AUPs. The Internet grew up in academic institutions, and in general, they have had the longest history of making the Internet available to their patrons. The remainder of this chapter will focus on the development of acceptable use policies by school and public libraries, where Internet access is less than five years old, if it exists at all.

Like their academic sisters, some school and public libraries have incorporated appropriate use of Internet resources into the library's policy for computer usage. Others have chosen to remind users that they must follow the appropriate use guidelines set forth by the library's regional Internet provider. Others have debated whether it's possible simply to apply their school district's policies or the library's policy and/or the American Library Association's principles on access to materials to the diverse array of resources accessible through the WWW. Generally, however, public and school libraries have chosen to draft new policies to focus on the specific issues that providing public access to the Internet fosters. In some instances, libraries have been required to have an AUP in place before they could begin providing public Internet access.

One of the main concerns for school libraries, and the most difficult issues for both public and school libraries to resolve, has been determining how to accommodate parental concerns for the offensive or objectionable items their children may access through the Web without compromising the library's mission to promote freedom of speech, the right to read, unrestricted access to information, and other intellectual freedom principles. The following section examines how school libraries have attempted to address these issues through the development of Internet AUPs.

AUPS AND SCHOOL LIBRARIES

In August 1994, before Internet use by children had become a politically hot topic, the Minnesota Coalition Against Censorship (MCAC) urged school officials providing Internet access to children to avoid attempting to control the Net environment, and instead, focus on instilling "individual users with the understanding and skills needed to use the Internet in ways appropriate to their educational needs." An admirable example of a policy espousing principles of librarianship and intellectual freedom, the MCAC's *Internet Statement* adamantly opposes any techniques to prevent students from accessing information "that some have identified as controversial or of potential harm to students;"

> Such schemes include: using coded account identifiers for students, restricting certain databases and sources of information to accounts identified as educational, limiting accounts to teachers, having owners and operators of information services screen access and communication, or having students voluntarily impose restrictions on themselves in exchange for the privilege of having an Internet account. Any of these strategies restrict student access to information or ability to communicate and should not be used by school officials or other agencies responsible for providing Internet access.

The MCAC endorses the *Minnesota Public School Internet Policy*, which takes a very proactive approach to children using the Internet by insisting that "Internet use guidelines should have as their underlying value the preservation of student rights to examine and use all information formats and should not be used to place restrictions on student use of the Internet." In addition to affirming that "Students have the right to examine a broad range of opinions and ideas in the educational process, including the right to locate, use and exchange information and ideas on the Internet" the policy insists that "school officials must respect a student's right to privacy in using Internet resources and using the Internet as a vehicle for communication." At the same time it supports students' rights to use the Internet without restrictions, the *Minnesota Public School Internet Policy* reminds them of their responsibilities "for the ethical and educational use of their own Internet accounts" and "to respect the privacy of other Internet users."

Integrating AUPs with Existing Policies

One of the main objectives for school districts developing acceptable use policies for Internet use within their schools is to integrate this policy with other school rules and procedures. The *Minnesota Public School Internet Policy* emphasizes this point by insisting that "policies and procedures to handle concerns raised about Internet resources should be similar to those used for other educational resources." Because a student's use of the Internet is linked to educational objectives, many schools have begun to incorporate guidelines for appropriate use of the Internet into existing school board policies.

"When I drafted our policy," says Jamieson McKenzie, technology director for Bellingham (Washington) Schools, "I found that AUPs were usually too narrow in scope and did not adequately address policy issues such as the curriculum, the role of teachers, the rights as well as the responsibilities of students and families." Students and others accessing the Internet through the Washington state schools are obligated to abide by the acceptable use policies of WEDNET, the district's regional Internet provider. However, as McKenzie explains in *From Now On*, a monthly electronic commentary on educational technology, board policies, while echoing the content of regional network AUPs, should "tie those standards to the district policies on student rights and responsibilities, drawing connections, for example, with the district policy and procedures on locker searches and a student's rights to privacy of freedom of speech. They tie consequences and procedures to those already in effect."

When Carl Zager, Technology Coordinator for the Monroe County (Indiana) Community School District, needed to establish an Internet acceptable use policy, he found the Bellingham Board Policy on the Web and used it as a model. Although McKenzie's Board Policy had been independently produced at the urging of the school district superintendent, Zager's motivation for developing an AUP had been spurred by a directive from the Indiana State Department of Education requiring all public schools to submit an acceptable use policy to the State in order to be eligible to receive state-supported funding for their Internet access.

In the late spring of 1995, the State Department of Education and the Indiana Governor's Office developed requirements and accompanying recommendations for *Public School Internet Acceptable Use Policies and Guidelines* to help prepare schools for Internet access, according to Mark Whitman, project consultant to Access Indiana, an Indiana statewide networking initiative, and one of the people instrumental in developing the state's Internet guidelines. Before a school's application for a state grant will be considered, the school corporation must have a local school board-approved AUP on file that complies with the state's policies and guidelines.

Announcement of the state's proposed AUP guidelines coincided with the July 3, 1995, *Time* magazine "Cyberporn" cover story on Internet pornography, and Whitman acknowledges that the media's negative portrayal of the Internet influenced the state's decision to require school districts to have an AUP. Media coverage "was quite a major factor—a real stimulus," Whitman says, while recognizing that the coverage was exaggerated. "Anybody who uses the Net regularly knows how overblown it was."

Nevertheless, Whitman and Mike Huffman, director of Educational Information Systems at the Indiana Department of Education, felt that an AUP could help protect local school districts. Huffman says:

> It seemed prudent that if the state were to take action in funding projects, that there be some assurance that common sense guidelines had been adopted. I'm certain that if left to their own devices, and with lots of time to investigate the issues and to gain some Internet experience, local school boards would have come up with similar requirements for students and staff. . . . In addition, having the guidelines in place from day one helps ensure that schools' use of the Internet would be less likely to suffer major setbacks because of problems that might occur in the absence of a policy. In general, the AUP represents sound fiscal and program policy. Schools may make it more stringent if they choose, but the state document establishes a common sense level of expectations and protects the students and the schools.

Although state departments of education do not typically *require* public schools to have Internet AUPs in place as Indiana does, most do *encourage* their K-12 schools to adopt them, and Huffman's remarks reflect reasons why most agencies, including libraries, choose to develop AUPs. (*Note:* As of February 1996, neither Huffman nor Whitman were aware of any other State Departments of Education that require their school districts to have an AUP in place. Efforts to determine whether any other state has such a policy have proved inconclusive. However, of the 15 responses we received to an e-mail survey distributed to K-12 network administrators within U.S. Departments of Education, none insisted that local public schools adopt a policy.)

Policies for Internet use in K-12 schools share characteristics of AUPs in general in their aim to educate students and their parents about the Internet and its instructional role, define students' eligibility for use, and outline conditions for appropriate use. Two issues typically cause debate, however: whether the school district should insist that only students with signed permission forms from their parents or guardians may access the Internet and how school educators should monitor student Internet use.

The Indiana state-developed *Internet Acceptable Use Policies and Guidelines* strongly recommends that students read and sign their school districts' AUP, but it does not require it. The guidelines do insist, however, that schools notify parents of their child's ability to access the Internet through school accounts and offer the option to request alternative activities not involving Internet access. And although Indiana also requires that a professional staff member supervise a student's use of the Internet, it emphasizes that students' educational use of the Internet is really the joint responsibility of students, parents, and school employees.

The state settled on this position, Whitman explains, because "We didn't want parents expecting that students were 100 percent protected from objectionable materials [just because the policy was in place]. We couldn't guarantee that following the policy would ensure appropriate student use, and we needed to make sure parents know that we can't be held accountable."

To help ensure that parents would be fully informed of their child's access to the Internet in school, MCCSC decided to have parents sign the school district's policy for *Student Access to Networked Information* and return it to the school. But the question of how to supervise student use of the Internet was not so easily decided. School board members debated at length whether they should require students and teachers to keep a "log" of individual student's use of the Internet. Concerned that items on the Internet have not been selected or determined appropriate for student use the way materials in the school library have been, one board member felt they should be able to track student use as a means of accountability, in case illegal behavior or violations to the policy occurred.

Zager argued that logging and note-taking were really instructional issues and was reluctant to interfere with how teachers might choose to use the Internet as a learning tool. He also couldn't guarantee the accuracy of software that automatically logs the Web sites a student visits, nor its ability to prevent students from accessing objectionable materials. Instead, he favored educating students about appropriate use of information resources, beginning in the early elementary grades, and relying on the school district's discipline policies based on principles of individual responsibility.

Ultimately, the MCCSC school board and Zager compromised by allowing the policy to include logging and note-taking methods as options for supervising student access of Internet resources. The final guidelines addressing this matter read: "a) Monitoring may include, where developmentally and instructionally appropriate, the keeping of manual logs by student users. b.) The MCCSC may apply technical means which attempt to regulate access to inappropriate information or which attempt to provide a "log" of accessed locations." Students violating any of the acceptable use principles outlined in MCCSC's *Policy 2521: Student Access to Networked Information Resources* will be disciplined according to existing policies and guidelines for Student Conduct, Student Discipline and Student Harassment rules. But with efforts to draw on existing policies to help dictate acceptable use of the Internet comes the realization that the school is treading new territory. Zager, who spent long hours discussing issues of concern with board members, and months refining the district's policy until it met the approval of all involved, reminded the board that it can always revise policies for Internet use "as we find out what works, and how it works."

An ongoing aspect of evaluation will consider whether the policies for Internet use comply with principles of intellectual freedom and students' academic rights. "Policies are created so that institutions will be protected, but they can mean a loss of academic freedom," Zager reflected. " . . . Although, I'm not sure how much academic freedom K-12 schools have had, anyway."

Preserving Student Rights

M. Guy Durrant, Technology Director for the Daggett School District in Utah, also has wrestled with this question and wonders whether it's possible for schools to uphold Internet users' rights of confidentiality and privacy in the K-12 environment, as the ALA's statement on *Access to Electronic Information* advises.

"There is no anonymity in accessing Web or gopher sites, or using newsnet services, since this kind of usage is quite trackable by IP address," he notes. And although school librarians don't typically follow students around the library noting all the materials they pull from the shelves as they search for information for a school report, Durrant says, "most school libraries would not have in their collection the kinds of materials which can be rather easily found on the Web . . . This may well be a case where the students' desire or privilege of privacy will give way to expediency. The school's need to monitor may be a more compelling interest than the student's wish for privacy."

In an effort to ensure appropriate educational use of the Internet, some schools have gone so far as to connect the Internet accessible terminal in the media center to a TV monitor and face it toward the media center's office—certainly a violation of privacy, even if students are informed of the practice.

Many school AUPs, such as the one implemented by the Newark Memorial High School in California, explicitly state that students may use the Internet for educational purposes only, to work on teacher-assigned research projects. School Librarian Nina Stull explains:

> The reason we have the students print out their history is for our "proof" that the students have stayed within the educational boundaries of the use of the Internet. We consider the Internet station a privilege to use. If we are challenged as to student use, we would be able to produce a list of sites our students accessed. We do not circulate the history, but store it for future reference if needed. The students have not felt it was an invasion of their

privacy, but have felt it proved, also, that they were following the school's Internet policies.

The Newark High School AUP also requires that students take an online "tour" of the Internet and have a parent/student signed AUP on file. Students are expected to pass the test that concludes the tutorial introducing them to key cyberspace concepts before they can use the Internet workstations.

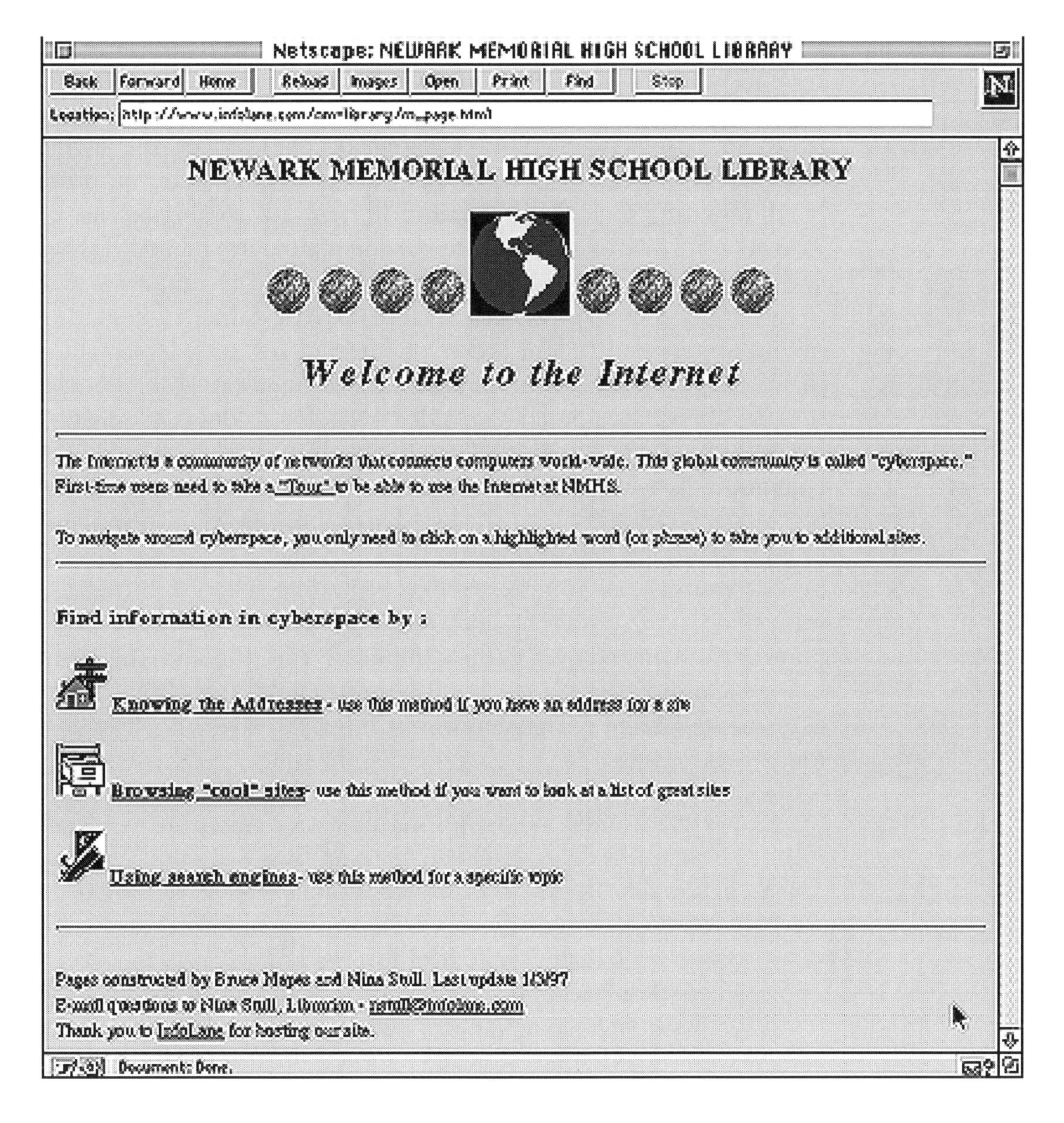

Figure 3.2
The Newark Memorial High School Library Home Page Begins with an Online Tour

Granting Internet access only to students who have obtained parental permission is another practice that runs counter to ALA principles on access to library resources. The American Library Association's *Access to Resources and Services in the School Library Media Program Interpretation of the LIBRARY BILL OF RIGHTS* states that "Major barriers between students and resources include . . . requiring permissions from parents or teachers." Nevertheless, parental permission slips approving a child's use of the Internet is found in nearly all school policies for Internet use.

"There really is no strong legal justification for such an agreement," Nancy Willard, an Internet Technology Consultant in Eugene, Oregon, explains in *A Legal and Educational Analysis of K-12 Internet Acceptable Use Policies*. "Students are expected to follow the district disciplinary policies without signing an agreement. On the other hand, requiring such an agreement will reinforce the importance of following the district policies, ensure adequate parental notification, and may assist in limiting liability for the district."

Evie Funk, a media specialist at Hopkins West Junior High in Minnesota, supervises student access of Internet resource by installing the Netscape Web browser on computer terminals near the circulation desk/work area on an as-needed basis for students conducting research. This way, library staff can easily observe students using the computers. Teachers also bookmark useful sites. Funk's school is one of the few K-12 schools which has decided not to require students or parents to sign any permission slips or policy statements governing Internet use. A letter to parents regarding school Internet use was placed in the parent newsletter and guidelines for student computer use are posted next to the computers. But, she says, the Technology Committee chose *not* to implement any signed user agreements, parent permission forms, Internet driver's licenses, etc. for several reasons:

1. No one wanted to take responsibility for gathering hundreds of signed policies and keeping them filed.
2. It seemed like it would be an administrative nightmare to keep track of signed policies, driver's licenses, etc. We all have more work than we can handle already!
3. There didn't seem to be any way we could *guarantee* that the only students doing independent searches would be students with signed policies on file. Often there are small groups of students gathered around computers or students are seated side by side in close proximity.
4. We spot check the Internet stations frequently, we educate the students about expectations, and our guidelines are clearly posted.

5. Most of the Internet searching is done in a "classroom" setting. It is focused on a specific curriculum topic, and is supervised by teachers and/or library staff.
6. Our community expects our school to provide Internet access. One of the main reasons they passed our technology bond referendum was so students would have access to online resources. After spending thousands of dollars on fiber-optic cabling, network wiring, and computers, it's seems like a waste of effort to provide barriers and "hoops to jump through" so that the students can access the resources.

Students who do not comply with the posted guidelines will be disciplined according to the existing behavior policies and regulations in our school. We have District support for this plan. Thus far," she says, "things are progressing smoothly. A couple of students have lost computer privileges for minor "hacking" activities, and some students whine and argue about who's turn it is to use the Internet stations, but so far, that's about all. We may have to re-evaluate this policy if unforeseen difficulties come up.

Because access to the World Wide Web and its multimedia resources is still new to most school libraries, parental reaction to Internet AUPs, pro or con, hasn't been widely reported. The only opposition Charles Hill, assistant superintendent for instruction and personnel for the Putnam Valley School District in New York, experienced to his district's policy for student use of the Internet came from the parent of a ninth grader who felt that requiring students and parents to sign an Internet acceptable use policy was unnecessary. "She felt that middle school students were old enough to use the Net in a reasonable manner without having to sign an Internet use policy, and that we should have faith in them," Hill explains. "I do not disagree with this position. But I also feel that we need to be clear about what our expectations are and make sure that both students and parents understand them."

To view examples of Acceptable Use Policies from K-12 Schools, follow these steps:

1. Open the CD-ROM and go to the Table of Contents page.
2. Click **Acceptable Use Policies**.
3. Scroll down to the "K-12 School Policies" subheading, which appears near the middle of the page.
4. Click the AUP you'd like to see.

AUPS AND PUBLIC LIBRARIES

The desire to inform patrons about expectations for use of computer and Internet resources underscores public library AUPs as well. Although public and school libraries share many of the same concerns, the main difference between public and school library Internet AUPs is that public librarians do not act in *loco parentis*. Public librarians are not responsible for supervising a child's or young adult's selection and use of materials in the library. This role is meant for parents, and most public library Internet policies clearly explain this by asserting, as does the Berkeley Public Library's Internet Use Policy:

> The Berkeley Public Library does not monitor and has no control over the information accessed through the Internet and cannot be held responsible for its content. As with other library materials, restriction of a child's access to the Internet is the responsibility of the parent/legal guardian.

This policy reflects the American Library Association's position on *Free Access to Libraries for Minors*, which states that librarians and governing bodies should maintain that only parents can restrict the access of their children to library resources. Parents who do not want their children to have access to certain library services should so advise their children. Librarians and governing bodies cannot assume the role of parents or the functions of parental authority in the private relationship between parent and child. Librarians and governing bodies have a public and professional obligation to provide equal access to all library resources for all library users.

The Lawrence (Kansas) Public Library incorporates this position, defining the responsibility parents have for supervising their child's use of library materials, in its *Internet Access Guidelines*:

> All Internet resources accessible through the Library are provided equally to all library users. Parents or guardians, **not** the Library or its staff, are responsible for the Internet information selected and/or accessed by their children. Parents— and only parents—may restrict their children—and only their children—from access to Internet resources accessible through the Library. Parents are advised to supervise their children's Internet sessions.

The Lawrence Public Library's Internet policy also makes a point of explaining that the library does not censor materials or make any attempt to protect patrons from information they find offensive. It also advises patrons to be savvy information consumers and to question the validity of information they find on the Net.

ALA's *Access to Electronic Information, Services and Networks* policy statement explains that "Providing connections to global information, services, and networks is not the same as selecting and purchasing materials for a library collection. Determining the accuracy or authenticity of electronic information may present special problems." In educating patrons about the library's relationship to Internet resources, some libraries have attempted to incorporate this position into their AUPs. This sentiment appears most often as a disclaimer on a library's Web page along with the reminder to parents that they are the ones who must supervise their child's use of the Internet.

In addition to issuing such a disclaimer, some libraries attempt to ensure that a patron has read the library's AUP and agrees to abide by it by requiring patrons to sign the policy before using Internet terminals. This can be a labor-intensive strategy for promoting appropriate use of Internet resources, which some libraries have sought to minimize.

In its *Internet Access Policy*, the Morton Grove (Illinois) Public Library states that "the Library is not responsible for the content, accuracy or availability of any external sites linked to these pages." The library repeats this statement on its opening Web page, the default page appearing on Internet terminals within the library, introducing patrons to "The Internet at the Morton Grove Public Library." The first paragraph declares:

> Through the Library's Internet connection you have access to the full range of resources on the World Wide Web. Only the Web 'pages' with the Library's name at the top are provided and maintained by the Morton Grove Public Library. Everything else comes from other computers around the country and around the world. The Library has no control over, and is not responsible for, the availability or content of any of these remote sites.

After listing another caveat about remote sites and stating that the disruptions to computer use, services, and equipment will not be allowed, a large blue button appears at the bottom of the page with the phrase 'I accept the conditions stated above' on it. The on-screen instructions inform patrons that clicking on the blue button will indicate that they have acknowledged and understood the above statement and accept sole responsibility for their use of the Internet, including the text and images they display. The button serves as a hyperlink to MGPL's on-screen tutorial for learning how to navigate the World Wide Web. Libraries' efforts to teach people about the Web and how to use it will be discussed at greater length in the chapter on training. The significance of this Web page to Acceptable Use Policies is the convenient method used both to alert patrons to and solicit their compliance with the library's rules and guidelines for acceptable use of the Internet when accessed through library terminals.

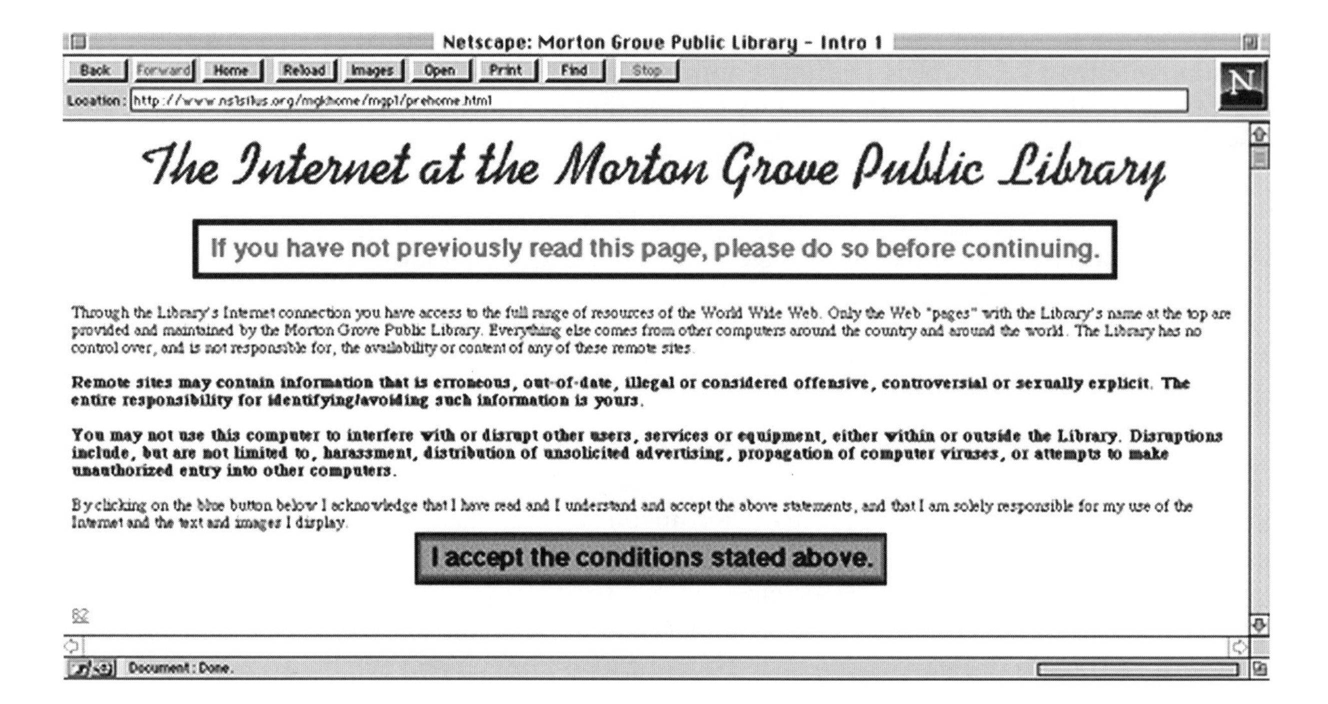

Figure 3.3
The "Pre-Home" Page of the Morton Grove Public Library Web Site Asks Patrons to Review and Accept Internet Usage Rules

Kevin Justie, Head of Technical and Automated Services for MGPL, acknowledges that the "pre-home page" cannot guarantee that users will read the library's advice and disclaimers for accessing the Internet, "but this seems the best we can do short of the unmanageable procedures and paperwork of keeping and checking some sort of waiver, or, in the case of kids, a permission slip."

Saint Joseph County Public Library also employs a default Web page briefing patrons on appropriate use of Internet terminals, in addition to posting its *Computer Usage Policy* at the terminals and at the reference desk. Initially, patrons had to sign an "Internet Sign-In" form at the reference desk, confirming that they had read and understood the SJCPL Computer Usage Policy and agreed that SJCPL assumed no liability for loss or damage to the user's data or for any damage or injury arising from invasion of privacy in the user's computer accounts, programs, or files. Patrons had to sign in to obtain a keyboard and mouse for the computer terminal.

The procedure was designed to prevent damage and loss of the equipment and to inhibit patrons from deleting internal computer files, explains Linda Broyles, Head of Reference at SJCPL. "If the user violates our policy, their signature is proof that they knew the rules ahead of time." But most importantly, she says:

> The sign-in slip allows us to regulate the time the user spends at a station. The Internet computers are in use from the time we open until we close. A certain percentage of users will sit all day if not monitored, and we wanted to give all patrons an equal chance. . . . Yes, we have users who try to circumvent the system, but for the most part it works, and works pretty smoothly I think. I would recommend it to any library with a small number of computers to monitor.

In May 1996, SJCPL installed a group of 12 Macintosh workstations in the reference department, with each one providing access to the library's OPAC, full-text magazine database, community database, newspaper index, and full Internet access. At that point, the library stopped holding keyboards at the reference desk and adopted a patron, self-regulated system.

Although the Berkeley Public Library (BPL) offers introductory online tutorials, it also asks patrons to read its *Internet Use Rules and Procedures* document, complete a Registration Form and pick up a copy of an Information and Tips sheet. Anyone under 14 is required to have a parent or guardian sign for them. "That's a policy we've always had for property liability," explains Internet consultant Carole Leita, a former Internet/Reference Librarian at Berkeley Public Library and creator of the library's Web site. To accommodate demand for computer access, the library requires patrons to sign up to use computers. Staff members also hold patrons' cards while they use the computer.

Although some librarians resent feeling like reservation clerks, Leita says, this procedure is no different from requiring patrons to register in advance for certain programs. The system also has proved beneficial in helping identify who was using the terminal when a problem occurred. Upon finding that one patron had moved his collection of erotic bookmarks into the middle of the kids file, Leita confronted the patron about the incident, explained that such actions would not be tolerated, and the problem did not happen again.

Having a policy in place will by no means guarantee that a library won't encounter problems. The New Castle Henry County Public Library (NCHCPL) in Indiana used a policy modeled after the one created by SJCPL. Patrons are required to read and sign the policy, which forbids accessing pornographic materials. But what *is* pornography, and what do you do when patrons within the library object to material that appears on screens others are using? NCHCPL administrators were forced to confront these difficult questions when a parent using a multimedia workstation with her daughter was appalled to see pictures of nude women appear on the screen of a nearby computer terminal being used by a young adult searching the Web. When the library board learned of the incident it imposed a temporary policy restricting all Internet access to patrons 18 or older, unless accompanied by an adult. The overly restrictive policy was lifted after the furor died down, but the library did consider using Internet filtering software on terminals in the Children's department.

"We did test Surfwatch and CyberPatrol," says NCHCPL Library Director Glenna Whitmill, "and we found the results very unsatisfactory." She explains that they encountered bugs and glitches that have been reported by the media. For example, if the word *breast* was blocked, they couldn't access information on breast cancer. And for some reason, when staff members conducted a search for *railroad*, they received a message that materials were blocked. Whitmill says she also had a library employee who is an experienced Web surfer try to download a movie that she would consider inappropriate for children. The employee was able to do so easily. Granted, Whitmill says, the employee was not a novice user, but this caused the greatest concern. "We were fearful that by installing this software we were in effect promising, 'it's safe'."

Realizing that using the software would not guarantee that children would not encounter material that may be considered inappropriate for minors, the library board decided not to purchase the filters. Instead, the board chose to implement more restrictive consequences for people who violate the AUP. Whitmill says she also plans to use a recommended list of children's sites as a "front end" or home page on the terminals in the Children's Department.

The Saint Joseph County Public Library in Indiana also received complaints from patrons about images they could observe displayed on library computer screens. In response to these complaints, SJCPL revised its *Acceptable Use Policy* to include the statement:

> Use of Library Internet access stations to display or disseminate sexually explicit or sexually suggestive (obscene/pornographic) material in any Library building is prohibited. Violators of this policy will be removed from the Library building and will have their library privileges revoked.

The library also decided to use the CyberPatrol blocking software. Although it does not indicate in its *Computer Usage Policy and Dis-*

claimer that the library uses this software, Linda Broyles, Head of Reference at SJCPL notes:

> Patrons are informed that CyberPatrol is in place when they hit a site that is blocked, and we are more than happy to explain our reasoning to them. We've been asked about it several times at the reference desk, and this is our response: 'We are using software that blocks sites that do not fit in with our selection policies.'

Donald Napoli, Director of SJCPL, who defended the library's ownership and circulation of Madonna's controversial *Sex* book, adds: " . . . our installation of filtering software has nothing to do with censorship. . . . Installing CyberPatrol has everything to do with why you're providing Internet access in the first place—for information. It is a matter of 'selection.'"

"When we initially provided Internet access for the public," Broyles explains, "we did not use blocking software nor did we have a statement prohibiting the display of sexually explicit materials. Both were implemented at a later date, out of necessity. The purpose of the policy is not for staff to 'spy' or 'check up' on patrons, but it will allow staff intervention if there is a complaint."

Other libraries have experienced similar problems and wondered how to respond to the irate patron unable to search the OPAC while another patron uses the computer terminal to peruse the latest supermodel's home page. Some libraries have alleviated this conflict by designating selected computer terminals as "Internet Only" or "OPAC Only" stations. Some explain that all patrons are eligible to reserve Internet terminals for an hour-long turn and the library does not monitor or judge the value of how a patron spends his or her time online. Although some librarians claim that blocking software enables them to "select" information resources, others view using such tools as a means of censoring an information resource. And whether or not they include statements in their Internet Policies advising patrons that the library cannot protect them from information or graphic depictions which they may consider offensive, most librarians would sympathize with the plight of patrons who don't want to feel accosted by images they can't help but see when in view of a computer terminal.

Bruce Flanders, director of the Lawrence Public Library in Kansas, related his experience with patrons viewing potentially offensive material on the library's public Internet terminals in a message to members of the publib-net LISTSERV:

> It has finally happened here . . . on Saturday, a patron sat at our Internet terminal much of the day perusing graphic nudity.

> Viewing of graphic nudity has happened before, but it didn't seem to cause any big concern and in fairness most of our Internet usage is for perfectly tame stuff.
>
> Some background: when we went online in June 1995 with public access to the Internet, we deliberately placed our Netscape browser-based public access Internet workstation in one of the most highly-trafficked areas of the library - right by the card catalog and the reference desk. We did so on purpose - so that no one would have the temerity to view a lot of 'dirty' pictures. Well, this patron was not fazed.
>
> I received three complaints today. One from a female patron who felt emotionally traumatized, another from a parent of teenage children, and another from a staff member who watched a couple shield the terminal from their much younger child.
>
> I feel torn—I don't want to limit access nor do I wish to introduce Surfwatch style censoring software. But, I don't want staff and patrons to feel abused by an insensitive lout—who may be back to repeat his all-day porno-thon. (It can be all-day in that there is no limit on usage unless someone else comes along to get in the queue.)
>
> My immediate reaction—not to change policies for access, but to reposition the workstation so that it is still near the reference desk but facing away from patrons. I also bought today an 'anti-glare' screen that pretty much shields a computer screen from anyone who is not directly in front of the screen. Obviously I am not so worried about glare as about patrons having stuff which they may personally find objectionable thrown into their path. This is admittedly an incremental step to deal with the problem. I hope it takes care of the problem so I don't have to resort to scaling back access.

The conflict points to the need for libraries to develop policies that preserve the rights of patrons to access potentially offensive, yet constitutionally protected, images and other forms of speech, while respecting the rights of other patrons who want to visit the library without subjecting themselves or their children to such images. As Virginia Rezmierski notes in her 1995 article *Computers, Pornography, and Conflicting Rights*:

> This is not about an individual's right to access material. It is about another individual's rights to choose not to access or be exposed to the material. This is about a small number of individuals intentionally intruding into the private, personal, work and psychological space of other people—to assert their power

> at the expense of another's while distorting and hiding behind First Amendment Rights.

It's a difficult dilemma to resolve. Although assessing when noise levels are disturbing to other patrons is a simple task for librarians, how do they determine whether the visual image one person is viewing on screen is intruding into the work space of other patrons? There are no clear guidelines for determining when the graphic display of images might be characterized as harassment. The way a library responds to this dilemma will depend a great deal on existing library policies, the current position of library administrators and board members, and community influences. Options range from reducing the ability of bystanders to see what's on a computer by installing or creating physical barriers between a computer screen and passive observers of images displayed, as the Lawrence Public Library did; to attempting to minimize the appearance of controversial graphic images by specifically prohibiting patrons from accessing certain kinds of materials, as the Saint Joseph County Public Library did by installing blocking software and forbidding users of its Internet access stations to display or disseminate sexually explicit or sexually suggestive (obscene/pornographic) material in the Library; to helping individual users understand the parameters of appropriate use of library computer resources by outlining the general terms of unacceptable use, as the Morton Grove Public Library describes on its "pre-home" screen:

> "You may not use this computer to interfere with or disrupt other users, services or equipment, either within or outside the Library. Disruptions include, but are not limited to, harassment, distribution of unsolicited advertising, propagation of computer viruses, or attempts to make unauthorized entry into other computers."

In addition to describing unacceptable use, some Internet policies appeal to the ethical considerations of their patrons by requesting their cooperation in respecting and sustaining the shared public environment the library provides. Staff members could refer to such policy statements should they feel compelled to ask patrons to cease viewing graphic images that have caused complaints. Rezmierski explains that this approach provides institutions with "an opportunity to lead through an educational effort—not to censor—but instead to proactively encourage individuals to think about the needs, rights, and values of others."

The Canby, Oregon, Public Library's *Internet Access Policy* asks users to "Be respectful of those around you and be aware that the use of the Internet, like all use of the library, falls under the library's conduct code." And the *Internet Access Policy* for the Oregon Public Electronic Network (OPEN), a community-based network administered by the City of Salem through the Salem Public Library, asserts:

> In keeping with Oregon and U.S. Constitutional guarantees, OPEN cannot restrict subscribers' rights of free expression. OPEN hopes that all subscribers will recognize that OPEN is a community based system reliant on wide acceptance and good will; please consider this and use good judgment when entering text and graphical materials into the system.

Whether adverse to imposing restrictions that conflict with intellectual freedom principles or aware that their best attempts to define inappropriate use will be open to some interpretation (considering that even the U.S. Supreme Court has failed to provide a clear definition of pornography), librarians can expect that the most thoughtful use policy will not preclude ongoing discussion about the library's responsibilities in providing fair and equitable Internet access for all users, and the need to teach staff members how to implement the policy effectively. Policies that strive to educate both library patrons and staff about the nature of the Internet and the library's objectives and principles, will foster informed debate, with the potential for examining this issue from all perspectives.

To view examples of Acceptable Use Policies from public libraries, follow these steps:

1. Open the CD-ROM and go to the Table of Contents page.
2. Click **Acceptable Use Policies**.
3. Scroll down to the "Public Library Policies" subheading, which appears toward the top of the page.
4. Click your selection.

WHAT SHOULD THE AUP COVER?

Should a library expressly prohibit patrons from using its computer terminals to display pornographic images or other forms of speech, which, although falling under First Amendment protections, are not materials most public libraries would consider adding to their collections? There are no easy answers. We hold that such a ban infringes on the rights of users to access constitutionally protected materials and therefore violates the *Library Bill of Rights*. We also support the American Library Association's position that the software "filters currently available would place the library in a position of restricting access to information that might be objectionable to some users. As such, they represent censorship, rather than selection." Ultimately, however, librarians must continue to be guided by their interpretations of existing library policies, input from community and board members, and, of course, by local, state, and federal laws.

Additional information about some of the inadequacies of blocking tools is available through "The Internet Advocate," included on the CD-ROM. Follow these steps:

1. Go to the Table of Contents and click on **Designing a Library Web Site**.
2. Click the link to **The Internet Advocate**, which appears near the bottom of this page under the subhead for "Example Resource Guides."

More links to information on filtering software appear in the Bibliography for Acceptable Use Policies on the CD-ROM. To get to that point, follow these steps:

1. Begin at the Table of Contents.
2. Click **Chapter Bibliographies**.
3. Click **Acceptable Use Policies**.
4. Choose the link you want to follow.

Is it even possible to craft a single, perfect, comprehensive AUP that will address all the potential conflicts that might occur when providing Internet access to the public? Not likely. As information technology and communications law evolves, unforeseen problems may arise. Internet AUPs can manage ongoing developments by relating guidelines for Internet use to the library's mission and to the library's policies concerning access to information, and by continuing to inform patrons about their rights and responsibilities as users of networked resources.

Although some are more detailed than others, Internet AUPs for libraries tend to address the same issues (security, illegal activities, ethical use, etc.) Defining a universally applicable policy is difficult because a good policy relates to the individual library's specific goals and mission. A library's efforts to adopt an Internet AUP also may be subject to the kinds of Internet resources it provides and guidelines established by affiliate agencies, such as a university computing center or a school board.

Nevertheless, some general principles apply. In all cases, be as clear and as specific as possible. Remember that you are addressing people who may be new to computers, much less the Internet. Thus, the first task should be to inform. Briefly explain what the Internet is and why your library has chosen to provide access. This is where the library has an opportunity to promote its mission and dedication to intellectual freedom. Next, discuss the responsibilities the library has as an access provider and then outline the responsibilities of the user of Internet resources, along with what the library considers unacceptable use. Be careful not to use overly vague, sweeping statements. Broad claims such as "There are information resources which are inappropriate to a library setting, thus librarians have the right to end Internet sessions" could easily tempt complaints about the most innocuous of materials and trap staff members in mediating on-the-spot arguments about what is "inappropriate." Remember that a good AUP will serve to guide both patron and staff behaviors.

Conditions for use often are included in a document separate from the actual policy. No matter how you outline the policy, it would be helpful for patrons to know who can use Internet terminals, what Internet resources are available, where the Internet terminals are located, when they are available, and how patrons can access them. If the library uses blocking software on any terminals, this also should be specified in the policy, with an explanation of why the library uses these tools. Finally, explain the consequences of unacceptable use. Let users know what will happen if they violate the AUP. Make it clear that even if the library does not actively monitor patrons' use of Internet terminals, staff members will intercede when informed of violations to the policy. Overall, the AUP should be crafted to promote, not inhibit, access to Internet resources.

With the above caveat and guidelines in mind, the following AUP template is geared toward Internet access in a public library. The CD-ROM includes examples of actual Internet AUPs from various kinds of libraries, along with pointers to other collections of policies. The ALA's interpretation of the Library Bill of Rights on Access to Electronic Information, Services, and Networks also is included on the CD-ROM.

AN AUP TEMPLATE

The following template appears on the CD-ROM at the top of the "Acceptable Use Policies" section. You can easily adapt this template for your own library, by saving it as a text file to a word processing program on your computer. Substitute the name of your own library for the italicized phrase *Your Library* in the following template.

To display the template, follow these steps:

1. Begin at the Table of Contents.
2. Click **Acceptable Use Policies**.
3. Scroll down to **Template for an Acceptable Use Policy** and click that link. The following template appears.

TEMPLATE: Internet Acceptable Use Policy for *Your Library*

Your Library's Reasons for Providing Internet Access

Your Library aims to develop collections, resources, and services that meet the cultural, educational, informational, and recreational needs of *Your* diverse community and which respond to advances in technology. With this goal in mind, and as part of its mission to meet the changing needs of the community, *Your Library* offers access to the Internet.

A worldwide network of computers, the Internet provides access to a wide range of educational, recreational, and reference resources, many of which are not available in print, but there is no central control over its content or users. The Internet also contains sexually explicit material and other information resources which you may consider objectionable or offensive. *Your Library* does not use filtering software to block access to information resources and cannot protect you from information or graphic images that you may find offensive. *Your Library* does not control the content of information that resides on the Internet, nor does the library monitor what Internet resources patrons choose to view.

In accordance with the ALA's interpretation of the *Bill of Rights for Access to Electronic Information, Services and Networks*, Internet resources accessible through the Library are provided equally to all library users, regardless of age. As with other library materials, parents or guardians, not the library or its staff, are responsible for supervising their children's selection of information on the Internet. Parents—and only parents—may restrict their children—and only their children—from accessing Internet resources. We suggest that parents concerned about the types of materials available on the Internet work with their young children as they explore Internet sites and help them select resources consistent with their family's values and boundaries.

Your Library can only be held accountable for information that appears on the World Wide Web pages produced by the Library. These are identifiable by the "*YL*" initials that appear in the upper left corner of the computer screen. Like other information resources, not all sources on the Internet provide accurate, complete, or current information. You need to be a good information consumer, questioning the validity of the information you find.

Responsibilities of *Your Library* as a Provider of Internet Access

Your Library will inform you of the Internet resources available to you through *YL* and provide basic instruction for how to access these resources. [*List here the Internet resources the library makes publicly accessible e.g.: FTP, Gopher, Telnet, Usenet newsgroups, and the World Wide Web. Does the library provide e-mail accounts for patrons? If not, explain how patrons can obtain personal e-mail accounts.*]*Your Library* will provide basic instruction to help you access Internet resources, but please understand that Internet-trained staff may not always be present to assist with your needs.

Consistent with its mission and service roles, *Your Library* will develop Web sites and other guides to Internet resources of particular usefulness and interest to the community. As part of the maintenance of the computer system, *YL* regularly checks for viruses; however, we cannot be held responsible for any loss of data or damage to personal disks, nor for any personal damage or injury incurred as a result of using the library's computing resources.

In keeping with existing library policies, *Your Library* will protect your rights to privacy and confidentiality. *YL* keeps any communications that reside on its computer network confidential. In general, however, electronic mail is not secure, and networks are sometimes susceptible to outside interference. As part of normal system maintenance, network administrators do have the ability to monitor system activity, but *Your Library* does not reveal information about an individual's use of its computer resources unless compelled to do so by a court order.

Responsibilities of Users of *Your Library*'s Internet Resources

You have the right to access materials of your choosing and engage in constitutionally protected communications. Please limit your time on Internet terminals to 30 minutes when others are waiting, and remember that you are responsible for legal and ethical use of all networked resources. Inappropriate use includes, but is not limited to the following:

- Attempting to alter or damage computer equipment, software configurations, or files belonging to the library, other users, or external networks;
- Attempting unauthorized entry into the Library's network or to any other computer system;
- Libeling, slandering, or otherwise harassing others;
- Distribution of unsolicited advertising or propagation of computer viruses;
- Violation of copyright, software license agreements or communications laws.

Libraries rely on the cooperation of their users in order to efficiently and effectively provide shared resources and ensure community access to a diversity of information. *Your Library* strives to balance the rights of users to access a wide range of information resources with the rights of users to work in a public environment free from harassing sounds and visuals. We ask all our library users to remain sensitive to the fact that they are working in a public space shared by people of all ages, with a variety of information interests and needs.

When informed of any violations to this policy, *Your Library* will enforce the rules and responsibilities outlined above, and your right to use Internet resources will be suspended for a specified time, depending on the damage caused by your actions. You will be notified of the length of and reason for your suspension. Individuals using library computing resources for illegal purposes may also be subject to prosecution.

How Can Users Obtain Additional Information?

Access to the Internet is compatible with Your Library's endorsement of the Library Bill of Rights, the Freedom to Read, the Freedom to View, and Access to Electronic Information, Services, and Networks statements from the American Library Association and with Your Library's Collection Development & Materials Selection Policy and Mission Statement. These policies are accessible on the Web. If you have any questions about this Internet Acceptable Use Policy, or any of the library's policies, please ask a librarian.

Chapter 4

Training Library Staff and Patrons on Internet Use

INTRODUCTION

So the good news is that the library's Internet site is up and running. The server has been properly configured, the security is in place, the Web site has been designed to the satisfaction of the staff, the graphics are complete, the internal and external links have been selected and incorporated into the many pages that make up the library's Web presence, access policies have been set, and the accounts and/or passwords have been distributed to the different librarian and patron user groups. Time to sit back, relax, and watch as this new service dramatically increases the number of patrons coming through the library's doors, correct?

No.

There are still a number of important issues that should be resolved, ideally in advance of the ribbon cutting ceremony. Of these issues, one that will prove to be taxing for public librarians offering Internet access is the question of training. This issue must be clarified at several different levels. Initially, there is the question of whether the public library will take on the added responsibilities for training at all. The decision to become involved in training programs involves serious commitments of time, personnel, facilities, and, of course, money.

If the library does want to offer training, the training issue must be further explored. First, there is the question of the domain of training, or, in other words, training for whom? In the broadest terms, there are two groups of people who could be trained: librarians and library staff, and patrons. In this chapter, the section "Training for Librarians and Library Staff" is based on the assumption that the library has decided to provide in-house training. Similarly, the section "Training for Patrons" assumes that training for patrons will also be provided.

The next problem involves determining the content of training. Although some elements of the training process will cut cross both classes of Internet users, there are different components of training that are appropriate to one group but not the other. The section "Templates for Training Programs" outlines two templates that can be used to set up training programs for library staff and patrons.

Another consideration of training is that each domain requires different types of commitment in terms of time, equipment, and cost, all of which should be carefully considered before taking the plunge. The section "Templates for Training Programs for Patrons" considers these issues in terms of costs and benefits to the library of pursuing different training program options.

TRAINING FOR LIBRARIANS AND LIBRARY STAFF

Training for librarians and library staff should cover both the front stage and back stage skills needed for Web and other Internet work. The main front stage skills involve searching for and retrieving text, data, image, software, and other files on the Internet, primarily through the WWW. These skills also involve gaining familiarity with TELNET, FTP, and Gopher services, which are typically integrated into WWW browsers, although they can stand alone. Front stage skills are important because they involve the acquisition of a range of skills and knowledge necessary to become a sophisticated user of the library's Internet services and resources. The goal of this level of training is to provide librarians and library staff with the ability to integrate Internet networking into their jobs effectively and to prepare them for the questions that will arise as users begin to explore the Internet. For example, patrons may seek a librarian's help when trying to download files with strange extensions, such as *.gz* or *.ohqx*; this requires an understanding of file compression and decompression. This component of the training program will mirror that offered to patrons in many ways.

Focusing primarily on the library's WWW services and resources, it seems clear that librarians should be thoroughly familiar with the major search engines currently in use on the WWW and be able to distinguish among regular search engines, metasearch engines, and the newest type of search tool, the niche engine. This is analogous to the constant need for librarians to remain current with reference and other print-based searching tools. However, the problem of searching for digital information is simply stated by A. Leonard, author of *Where to find anything on the net*:

> Finding what you want on the Internet can be like looking for a needle in a haystack. Fortunately, about the only thing growing faster than the Net itself is the number of online search tools to help you track down whatever it is you're looking for. But which tool is really the best? Where should you go first?

Furthermore, as D. Jakob states in *Finding Information on the Web*:

> Internet users, like librarians, must realize when one resource discovery tool is more effective than another. Suppose a user does not know the general category (classification) for a particular term. Through a directory listing, the search may take a very long time. A searchable index could take the user directly to the right location. Directory listings might lead a user to access six or eight pages before linking to the desired resource, whereas a searchable index may require only two steps to arrive at that same resource. Knowing which tool to use is half the battle in finding information on the Internet.

In addition to knowing *how* to use the search tools, librarians should understand how the tools work, including their strengths and weaknesses. This will allow them to understand *when* to use a search tool, because all of the search tools currently available on the WWW are limited in different ways, and some are more appropriate for certain types of questions than are others. Webster and Paul point out that "surfing is fun when you have the time to explore, but when you have a patron standing by, or need to find a specific piece of information quickly, or need to find that same information again, surfing and serendipity soon lose their charm."

During training sessions, we typically require people to run the same query on at least three different search engines and compare the results. Without fail, this exercise engenders spirited discussion as people discover that certain engines do not turn up answers that others do and begin to explore the nuances of online searching for networked information. Perhaps the most important lesson comes with the realization that, like print reference sources, search engines have their strengths and weaknesses.

Metasearch engine: A type of search engine that takes a query and submits it to two or more search engines.

Niche engine: A kind of search engine that extensively searches a certain portion of the Internet. For example, there are niche engines that specialize in business information, chemical information, or English literature.

There is also a set of back stage skills that is critical in managing WWW sites. Training for librarians should include the fundamentals of working on WWW documents, from basic markup with HTML to the use of advanced HTML tags for tables, frames, image maps and forms; the latter may also require that someone in the library understand common gateway interface (CGI) scripting and database management. In addition to HTML markup, librarians should understand how to work with digitized images, sounds, and other forms of multimedia files. The goal of this portion of the training program is to allow librarians to create and maintain their own and "official" library pages on their WWW site whether the pages are mounted on their own library server or, if the library uses an Internet service provider, on a remote server. In addition, these skills allow librarians to work with patrons, instructing them in the use of HTML for pages which may be linked to the library's pages or mounted on patrons' personal accounts.

There is a set of pages on the CD-ROM explaining the basic elements of HTML markup. To view the information, follow these steps:

1. Open the CD-ROM and go to Table of Contents.
2. Click on **Training Options**.
3. From this page, click on **HTML Demonstration Page**.

If the library's Web sites are run on UNIX-based servers, there should also be training sessions for librarians explaining the intricacies of UNIX file management. The goal of this portion of the training program is to allow the library to create, organize, and maintain the content of their Web site. At a minimum, people who will be working on the library's Web site will have to understand how to create files and directories, how to copy and rename these files, how to work with a basic UNIX text editor such as *pico* or *vi* to create content and edit files, and how to move files from one directory to another. They should have a grasp of the commands needed to set file permissions so that WWW files have world-read access and restricted write access and they should know how to create links among files that are located in different subdirectories. If the library hosts its own server, the people responsible for maintaining it will have to acquire an additional set of technical skills, including installing and configuring the server software, setting up the main directories, establishing the correct file ownership and permissions to restrict access to the server and provide security for the site, writing server scripts, and managing the log files. They will also have to perform regular maintenance of the site, checking links for currency and adding and deleting content and links as needed. The detailed discussion of these skills becomes very technical very quickly and is beyond the scope of this chapter; see the Appendix B at the end of the book for references to works about learning UNIX and managing Web sites.

A third component of training involves acquiring the skills and knowledge necessary to train librarians, library staff, and patrons in the use of the library's Internet connection. The goal of this level of training is to "train the trainer." It has been our experience that Internet training sessions differ somewhat from other types of computer training because of problems like network traffic delays at local, regional, and national levels, general instability of many Web sites, the appearance and disappearance of links and content across the World Wide Web, and potential conflicts between Internet software and other software running on the computer all combining to introduce a healthy dose of unpredictability into the typical training session. The librarian-trainer has to consider more than simply the content of a particular training session.

A successful training program involves careful planning and preparation. After deciding how much time can be devoted to the entire training program and each session, trainers should carefully structure the activities for each session. There should be a mix of information presentation, handouts, discussion, and hands-on activities, with the bulk of time allotted to the latter. Each session should have clearly defined goals and objectives which should be explained to the participants at the beginning of the session and included in any materials that are handed out. The trainer should be completely familiar with the activity that participants will be doing in the session. If possible, the activities should be tested on the computers in the room that will be used for the training session; there can be differences in the way an activity will unfold which are caused by the platforms, operating systems, and versions of browser and other Internet software that have been installed on the training computers, and by the network connection in the training room.

When the activity involves the use of Internet services and resources, as in the case of a Web searching exercise, the trainer should run through the entire activity as close to the training session as possible. This serves two purposes. First, it ensures that the trainer will be thoroughly familiar with the activity. Second it allows the trainer to check that all the components of the activity are working; all the links are active, all the sites are operational, and all of the answers can be found.

Howard Rosenbaum uses a strategy for organizing a three-hour session which begins with approximately 10 to 15 minutes of information about the session, followed by two to two and a half hours of hands-on work, followed by discussion and wrap-up. Typically, when the introductory comments are concluded, he will run through an abbreviated version of the activity, such as marking up a paragraph or using a search engine, while participants follow along; then they are turned loose. While they are working, the trainer should be circulating around the room, stopping to check on and talk with each participant.

The one-to-one interaction is critically important to the success of the session; trainers should make a concerted effort to talk to every participant, even those who seem to be moving through the activity smoothly. After the activity is completed, the trainer should solicit comments from as many participants as possible; it is especially useful to encourage discussion of the range of problems that they experienced as they carried out the exercise. The discussion of problems and their resolutions can be an opportunity for learning. Rosenbaum has found that reiterating the goals and objectives at the end of the session is useful for participants, many of whom may be struggling to make sense of the experience. If possible, a 10:1 participant-to-trainer ratio should be maintained; this ensures that each participant can receive the trainer's individual attention. If the ratio must be higher, the trainer has to be aware of the need to interact with each participant at least once in each session. In such cases, Rosenbaum recommends using an assistant.

TRAINING FOR PATRONS

The Internet has become a popular topic for the mainstream media, and the days are long gone when Net access can be shrouded in mystery. However, despite the prevalence of information about the Internet, librarians cannot afford to assume that their potential users understand either information networking or computing; such an assumption will end up costing them in time and money as they struggle with the problems that novices and intermediate users have with navigation on the Internet. There is a clear need for training which can address the needs of these more typical users as they learn how to use the Internet. In broad terms, training for patrons covers content concerns and, equally important, attempts to anticipate the types of typical problems and uncertainties that patrons using the library's system can be expected to experience. With an understanding of the range of problems and difficulties that users may have, those responsible for training can develop more effective strategies for delivering the content of the training sessions.

Although it is sometimes thought that training for patrons can focus exclusively on the Internet and its services and resources, research by Hert, Rosenbaum, and their colleagues indicates that trainers must recognize that many users have a set of problems which do not originate in the Internet itself. There are difficulties that occur at the levels of the local workstation and the Internet service provider, the resolutions of which are part and parcel of successful Internet use. Such problems may be as simple as not knowing how to log on to the computer and as complex as not understanding the differences in file formats necessary for successful file decompression. In addition, trainers must be aware that novice users may be unable to determine the level at which their problems are occurring. Many times, the machinery (local and otherwise), resources, and services that are hidden behind the computer screen are perceived by the user as a single seamless system. This is a reasonable assumption, and one which represents an ideal realization of the Internet; it works, however, only so long as the user does not experience any problems.

In addition to these technical problems, users may also experience problems at a conceptual level. This type of problem can be typified by a confusion that many users have in which they cannot easily distinguish between the many different resources and services they encounter during a session on the World Wide Web. For example, users may not realize that they are using file transfer protocol (FTP) when they click on a link on a page they are browsing and a file begins to download. What kind of file is this? Where did it go? What do the letters at the end of the filename mean (*.zip*, *.gz.*, *.tar*)? This confusion occurs because of the seamless way that the protocol on which the Web is based integrates a wide range of existing protocols, including FTP, TELNET, and Gopher. Users can easily grasp the basics of using a browser, but many have never had occasion to use these other older protocols.

Another problem arises when users see messages from the browser that a particular link on a page cannot be accessed because the browser cannot find the software needed to open the link. Suddenly, users are confused by the distinction between the software that provides them with access to the Web and the software that is needed to see the content provided on Web pages, like audio, video, and multimedia. This occurs because browser software must be aided by an increasing range of supporting software—called *helper applications* and *plug-ins*—and these programs will be available only if the librarian has installed them. Training therefore needs to address these types of distinctions and confusions.

There is a set of pages on the CD-ROM that provides an excellent introduction to the World Wide Web. To view it, follow these steps:

1. Open the CD-ROM and go to the Table of Contents.
2. Click on **Training Options**.
3. Click on the **University of Houston Libraries WWW Tutorial**.

Dr. Carol A. Hert and Dr. Howard Rosenbaum, professors of Library and Information Science, and their colleagues found that users need help locating information, using applications (logging in, using commands, etc.) and determining the utility of the information retrieved. Their findings indicate that users have a tendency to blame themselves when problems arise (for example, they are making mistakes or they lack understanding of the system). Trainers must remember the affective elements of training and provide positive reinforcement to users so that they continue to have productive learning experiences. They must repeatedly explain to users that trial and error, or learning through mistakes, is one of the most valuable ways to learn to us e the Internet. (See the Frequently Asked Questions table inside the front cover of this book for information on questions new users often ask). A comment that Rosenbaum has made over and over again in the training sessions he has conducted for librarians has become a workshop slogan: *Go ahead. Try it. You can't break the Internet. Worst case is that you reboot!*

Experience has also shown that a group training environment is a successful one. Although it is critical for the trainers to spend time with each individual in the session, as often as not, users are able to resolve their uncertainties though interactions with colleagues rather than the instructor. Additionally, allowing time for participants to experiment and make mistakes is part of a useful learning experience.

TEMPLATES FOR TRAINING PROGRAMS

Because the training for librarians and library staff includes that offered to patrons and "train the trainer" components, templates for two different types of patron training programs are presented in this section. Keep in mind that these templates have been the basis for successful training programs that have been used to introduce librarians to the Internet. They have been implemented under near ideal conditions; with state-of-the-art computer labs, two and sometimes three trainers, three hour modules, and groups of approximately 25 participants. These templates should be therefore considered as a menu from which can be drawn the arrangement of training modules that best fit the needs and available resources of the library.

Templates for a Training Program for Patrons

There are several strategies that can be used for training users, two of which will be presented in this section. The first is a program that provides users with a set of basic Internet skills involving the use of several different protocols and services (e-mail, TELNET, FTP, Gopher, and World Wide Web browsers). This type of program is useful if the library offers patrons an account on a mainframe computer or if patrons have this type of account with an Internet service provider. Typically the basic network services are available to users through their accounts without the use of a Web browser. This type of training can be offered as a service to users who may be struggling with personal Internet connections. The second type of program focuses primarily on the World Wide Web and covers the use of search engines and the basics of HyperText Markup Language (HTML). This program is useful if patrons will be using the library's Web site to explore the Internet and if they are allowed to create and mount Web pages, either on the library's server or through their own service provider.

> There is a set of pages on the CD-ROM that provides an excellent introduction to using and searching the World Wide Web. To view the pages, follow these steps:
>
> 1. Open the CD-ROM and go to the Table of Contents page.
> 2. Click on **Training Options.**
> 3. Then click on the **Morton Grove Public Library's "How to Navigate the World Wide Web Tutorial."**

The first version of a series of training sessions covers a complete set of skills needed to use the Internet for browsing and searching for and retrieving information. This session assumes that the user has the lowest level of connectivity: an account on a mainframe or minicomputer housed either in the library or at a commercial service provider. The objectives of this training are to provide the user with the ability to use the following:

- electronic mail for personal communication and computer conferencing;
- search tools, such as Telnet and Archie for locating information, services, and other resources; and
- resource discovery tools, such as file transfer protocol (FTP), Gopher, and World Wide Web browsers, such as Netscape, Internet Explorer, Mosaic or an Internet service's proprietary browser, for text, data, image, sound, and software retrieval.

Training Program Example #1

This training program is divided into six modules, each of which involves a different set of hands-on activities. After a brief introduction to the topics covered in the module, the trainer leads the users through directed exercises which are customized for the library or training center's system. The exercises should be designed to be covered in two hours, and the trainer should be completely familiar with the steps needed to complete the exercise.

After the brief lecture, users begin to work on the exercises and the trainer circulates around the room, helping users work through the problems that arise. If possible a 10:1 trainee-to-trainer ratio should be maintained. This allows the trainer to spend sufficient time with each user; larger groups can certainly be trained in this program, but as the number of trainees increases, the amount of time the trainer can spend with each person decreases, leading to potential decreases in the quality of the experience for the trainees. Each module should be completed in three hours; these modules have been delivered in an intensive three-day workshop (two each day), in three weeks (one module twice a week), and in six weeks.

A typical schedule for this type of training program is described below. Each module is divided into the main *topics* that will be covered in the session, the *activities* that participants will do, and suggested *resources* that librarian-trainers can draw upon to gather background information and develop handouts. Note that this is a suggestive list of resources. No attempt is made to be comprehensive. Where possible, the resources are found on the Internet, which can reduce the cost of preparing these modules; the links to these resources were active as of April, 1997.

Module 1: Electronic mail and computer conferencing; LISTSERV, majordomo, LISTPROC, and other conferencing software, USENET

Topics:

What is the Internet?
Using electronic mail for private communication
Using electronic mail for computer conferencing on mailing lists (LISTSERVs, majordomo, LISTPROC, and others) and USENET newsgroups
Netiquette

Activities:

Sending and receiving e-mail messages
Finding computer conferences of interest
Searching LISTSERV archives
Reading, posting, and saving USENET newsgroup articles

Resources:

E-MAIL: A common e-mail program used on many UNIX systems is *PINE*. Here are two sources for more information about this program.

1. PINE (a UNIX mail program): The University of Washington's Pine Information Center is available at:
   http://www.cac.washington.edu/pine/
2. A PINE tutorial by M. Aldritch is available at:
   http://gpu.srv.ualberta.ca/~maldridg/Wiz/Wizard

Computer Conferences: There are hundreds of LISTSERV-, majordomo-, and LISTPROC-based computer conferences that people can explore during a training session. Here are five ways to locate a computer conference of interest that people can use in a workshop.

1. Send an e-mail message to:
   listserv@vm1.nodak.edu ~or~
   listserv@uga.cc.uga.edu ~or~
   listserv@kentvm.kent.edu
   The text of the message should read:
   list global /<*topic*> Replace <*topic*> with a single word.
   For example:
   list global/books
   There should be no subject line in the message or any other lines of text (not even a signature file).
2. There are postings on USENET groups with lists of LISTSERV conferences that can be downloaded. On USENET, find the newsgroup:
   news.lists
   and the regular posting:
   "Publicly_Accessible_Mailing_Lists" (14 parts)

3. Information about LISTSERVs is also available at FTP sites. Using FTP, go to:
   rtfm.mit.edu
   login: anonymous
   password: your e-mail address
   Then go to:
   /pub/usenet/news.answers/mail/mailing-lists
   And download the file "mailing-lists"
4. Information about computer conferences can be found on the World Wide Web at the E-Mail Discussion Groups/ Lists - Resources site:
   http://www.webcom.com/impulse/list.html
5. Searching LISTSERV archives: A useful document that will arrive as an e-mail message is available at:
   listserv@ubvm.cc.buffalo.edu
   The text of the message should read:
   GET MAILSER CMD NETTRAIN F=MAIL

USENET: If people have access to the Internet through a dial-in shell account and newsreader software or their Web browser is properly configured with the IP address of a USENET news server (ask your technical staff if these options exist on your system), they can access the world of over 12,000 Usenet newsgroups. Here are two ways to find more information about USENET:

1. On the Web, you can locate a USENET group of interest by searching the list available at:
   http://www.dejanews.com
2. A USENET tutorial is available at the Usenet Info Center Launch Pad:
   http://sunsite.unc.edu/usenet-i/

Module 2: Direct access to resources using remote login (TELNET)

Topics:

What is TELNET?

Using TELNET to access online public access library catalogs (OPACs), community networks, Freenets, and other resources and services

Activities:

Visiting one or more TELNET sites and critically reviewing them

Resources:

TELNET: TELNET is a useful protocol, particularly so for exploring library catalogs that are on the Internet. Here are three sources of information about TELNET:

1. On the Web, you can find a chapter from Brendan Kehoes's *Zen and the Art of the Internet*, 1st Edition, explaining TELNET at:
   http://sundance.cso.uiuc.edu/Publications/Other/Zen/zen-1.0_6.html #SEC59
2. Another TELNET resource is available at:
   http://tecnet0.jetejcs.mil:9000/./htdocs/utl/iis/CHAPTER6BIG.html
3. Another resource is the World Wide Web's Virtual Library page "TELNET Help," available at:
   http://www.commerce2000.com/logistics/wokltnh.htm

Module 3: Searching for people and resources

Topics:

Using TELNET to search for people with NETFIND and the "finger" command

Using TELNET to search for text, image, and software files with ARCHIE

Activities:

Searching for yourself using NETFIND

Searching for software and text files using ARCHIE

Resources:

Searching for information: Searching for information is becoming much more complex over time as more resources and search tools are set up on the Internet. Here is one source of information about searching for networked information:

1. A print source about searching is *The Internet Searcher's Handbook: Locating Information, People, and Software* by P. Morville, L. Rosenfeld, and J. Janes, (1996). New York, NY: Neal Schuman.

NETFIND: This is one of the older network resources that can be used to track down people's e-mail addresses. Here are two sources for information about NETFIND:

1. A useful page is "NETFIND: What is NETFIND," available at:
   http://www.mis.net/misnet/newuser/inetref/netfind.html
2. A Web-based link to NETFIND sites is at:
   http://www.internic.net/wp/netfind-servers.html

ARCHIE: This is one of the older tools that can be used to search for files in FTP archives all over the Internet. Here are three sources of information about ARCHIE:

1. There is a useful page on the Web, "ARCHIE: What is ARCHIE," available at:
   http://www.earn.net/gnrt/archie.html
2. An "ARCHIE Server list" is available at:
   http://ns.kren.nm.kr/Internet/Service/list/archie-list.html
3. The document "A Sample Archie Search With An Archie Client" is available at:
   http://www.swifty.com/VB/cone/files/archie/archsamp.html

Module 4: Retrieving files from the Internet

Topics:
What is File Transfer Protocol (FTP)?
Using FTP to retrieve text, image, and software files
Downloading and accessing files: File formats and file compression and decompression

Activities:
Retrieve the files located in the ARCHIE search
Decompress and display the files

Resources:
FTP: File transfer protocol can be used to retrieve text, image, audio, video, and multimedia files and software. Downloading files is half the struggle. Dealing with file compression and decompression is the other half. Here are four sources of information about FTP:

1. On the Web, a page with useful information "Anonymous FTP Frequently Asked Questions (FAQ) List, V. 5.0; last modified May 21, 1996" is available at:
   http://www.cs.purdue.edu/homes/veygmamk/ftp-faq.html
2. The Robert A.L. Mortvedt Library - Pacific Lutheran University has an online guide INTERNET: FILE TRANSFER PROTOCOL (FTP).
   http://medisg.stanford.edu/hypertext/net/dummy_guide/bdgtti-1.02_11.html#SEC119
3. Another resource on FTP is available at:
   http://www.december.com/net/tools/nir-tools-ftp.html
4. A source for information on file compression is Patrick Crispen's "MAP16: FTP FILE COMPRESSION," available at:

http://bcn.boulder.co.us/help/Roadmap/msg23.html

Module 5: Using resource discovery and retrieval tools [I]

Topics:
What are Gopher and Veronica?
Using Gopher and Veronica to search for and retrieve text files

Activities:
Use Gopher and Veronica to answer a set of questions

Resources:
GOPHER: This network resource provided many people with a new way to organize and present digital information on the Internet using software that was developed at the University of Minnesota and given away for free. Here are two sources of information about GOPHER:

1. The main GOPHER site is at the University of Minnesota and is available at:
   gopher://gopher.tc.umn.edu/
2. A well-organized set of pages "EFF's Extended Guide to the Internet: Gophers, WAISs and the World-Wide Web" is maintained by the Electronic Frontier Foundation (EFF), available at:
   http://www.eff.org/papers/eegtti/eeg_185.html#SEC186

VERONICA: This is the search tool that was developed at the University of Nevada-Reno which enables people to search for information on GOPHER servers anywhere on the Internet. Here is a source for information about VERONICA:

1. An FAQ file about VERONICA is "Common Questions and Answers about veronica, a title search and retrieval system for use with the Internet Gopher," available at:
   gopher://gopher.unr.edu/00/veronica/veronica-faq

Module 6: Using resource discovery and retrieval tools on the World Wide Web [II] (Lynx, Netscape, Internet Explorer, Mosaic)

Topics:
What is the World Wide Web? What is a browser?
Using browsers to explore the Web (Lynx, Netscape, Internet Explorer, Mosaic)
Using search engines to locate text, image, software, and multimedia files on the Web

Activities:

Use WWW search engines to answer a set of questions

Resources:

WORLD WIDE WEB: There are many sources about the World Wide Web, both in print and on the Web. Only one is mentioned here, because it is a site maintained by the people who created the Web. This is an excellent starting point to find other useful pages about the Web.

1. The World Wide Web Consortium maintains a set of pages "About The World Wide Web and the Web Community" with introductory information about the Web, available at:
   http://www.w3.org/pub/WWW/WWW/

WWW SEARCH ENGINES: The key to directed use of the Web is the search engine. New search engines are appearing weekly, and existing ones are continually being improved. Here are four sites that are jump-off points to other information about search engines:

1. A collection of print and Web-based "Literature about search services" is maintained by T. Koch and is available at:
   http://www.ub2.lu.se/desire/radar/lit-about-search-services.html
2. A sites with links to many WWW search tools is "SearchIT," at Northwestern College, available at:
   http://www.netins.net/showcase/nwc-iowa/
3. Another site that allows you to search many engines is the World Wide Web Launchpad - Search Engines, available at:
   http://www.flex.net/~greg/launch.htm
4. A lengthy listing of search engines can be found on "Dr. Webster's Big Page of Search Engines, available at:
   http://www.123go.com/drw/search/search.htm

TRAINING PROGRAM EXAMPLE #2

The second version of a training program covers a set of skills needed to use the World Wide Web browsers for browsing and searching for and retrieving information. This program assumes that the user has a higher level of connectivity through the use of a browser (Lynx, Netscape, Internet Explorer, or Mosaic) on a mainframe or minicomputer housed either in the library or at a commercial service provider. The objectives of this training are to provide the user with the ability to use the following:

- many of the search engines that allow them to submit queries and retrieve information on the World Wide Web;
- browsers for resource discovery and retrieval of text, data, image, sound, and software files;
- HTML markup language (including tables and frames) to exploit the possibilities of the Web and allow users to become publishers of networked information.

This training program is divided into eight modules, each of which involves a different set of hands-on activities. After a brief introduction to the topics covered in the module, the trainer leads the users through directed exercises which are designed to lead the user through the intricacies of using the Web. As before, the exercises should be designed to be covered in two hours, and the trainer should be completely familiar with the steps needed to complete the exercise. Each module should be completed in three hours; these modules have been delivered in three weeks (one module a day, twice a week), and in six weeks. A typical schedule for this training protocol is as follows:

Module 1: Searching the World Wide Web (exploring search engines)

Topics:

What is the World Wide Web and what can we do with it?

Using search engines (single search engines, metasearch engines, and niche search engines)

Comparison of search engines

Activities:

Using several different search engines to answer a set of questions

Resources:

WWW SEARCH ENGINES: The key to directed use of the Web is the search engine. New search engines are appearing weekly, and existing ones are continually being improved. Here are two sites that are jump-off points to other information about search engines.

1. A collection of print and Web-based "Literature about search services" is maintained by T. Koch and is available at:
   http://www.ub2.lu.se/desire/radar/lit-about-search-services.html
2. A list of sites with links to many WWW search tools is "SearchIT," at Northwestern College, available at:
   http://www.netins.net/showcase/nwc-iowa/

Module 2: Basic HTML Markup

Topics:

What is HyperText Markup Language?

What are the basic elements of HTML? (paired and unpaired tags, links)

How do we create and markup pages for the World Wide Web using HTML?

Activities:

Begin marking up a resume or some other document with basic HTML tags and hypertext links (to other documents on the Web, other documents in the same collection of Web pages, and within the same page)

Resources:

BASIC HTML MARKUP: There are many sources, both in print and on the World Wide Web, that provide basic information about and instruction in HTML markup. Here are six resources about basic HTML markup:

1. The World Wide Web Consortium maintains a set of pages "HyperText Markup Language (HTML)," available at:
   http://www.w3.org/pub/WWW/MarkUp/
2. A set of "HTML Markup Demonstration Pages" is maintained by H. Rosenbaum and is available at:
   http://php.ucs.indiana.edu/~hrosenba/DemoCon.html
   Note: These are available on the CD-ROM accompanying this book.
3. The Maricopa Center for Learning and Instruction has "Writing HTML: A Tutorial for Creating WWW Pages," available at:
   http://www.mcli.dist.maricopa.edu/tut/
4. K. Werbach maintains a set of pages devoted to HTML markup called "The Bare Bones Guide to HTML," available at:
   http://werbach.com/barebones/
5. A good print source for basic HTML markup is *HTML for the World Wide Web*, 2nd Edition, by E. Castro, (1997). Berkeley, CA: Peachpit Press. Chapters 1, 2, 4, and 10.

Module 3: More HTML

Topics:

What are some other ways of using HTML to present information? (lists)

How do we work with color and images?

Activities:
Continue marking up resume using lists, images and colors

Resources:
INTERMEDIATE HTML: After becoming familiar with basic markup, the next step is to learn how to use lists, images, and color. Here are two sources about these features of HTML markup:

1. A useful set of pages, "Welcome to the HTML Station," is maintained by J. December, available at:
   http://www.december.com/html/
2. *HTML for the World Wide Web*, 2nd Edition, by E. Castro, (1997). Chapters 3, 5, and 8.

Module 4: Using HTML to create tables

Topics:
How can HTML be used to display information in a table?
What are the basic components of table markup?

Activities:
Incorporate tables into the resume

Resources:
TABLES: Tables are a useful addition to HTML markup, offering much greater control over page layout. Here are three sources with information about tables:

1. A complete explanation of "Tables as implemented in Netscape 1.1" is maintained by Netscape Communications, available at:
   http://home.netscape.com/assist/net_sites/tables.html
2. Another useful resource is "Tables For Your Home Page," maintained by *PC Magazine*, available at:
   http://www.pcmag.com/issues/1418/pcm00084.htm
3. *HTML for the World Wide Web*, 2nd Edition, by E. Castro, (1997). Chapter 6.

Module 5: Using HTML to create frames

Topics:
How can HTML be used to display information in frames?
What are the basic component of frames markup?

Activities:

Create a frames-based version of the resume

Resources:

FRAMES: Frames are a recent addition to HTML extensions. They provide a very different way to present information in a browser because the window can be divided into a number of smaller frames, each displaying different information. Here are three sources about frames.

1. A set of pages about "Frames: An introduction" is maintained by Netscape Communications, available at:
   http://home.netscape.com/assist/net_sites/frames.html
2. J. Lichtman maintains "Jay's Guide to Frames," available at:
   http://www.columbia.edu/~jll32/html/frame.html
3. C. Rose maintains a set of pages "Netscape Frames," available at:
   http://www.newbie.net/frames/

Module 6: Advanced HTML [I]: Forms

Topics:

What is a "form" and what is it used for?
What are the basic components of forms markup?

Activities:

Create a form that is linked to the resume

Resources:

FORMS: With forms, Web pages can become interactive. People can send information to the creator of the Web page by filling out and submitting information on a form. Here are four sites with information about forms:

1. The World Wide Web Consortium has a page about "The FORM element," available at:
   http://www.w3.org/pub/WWW/MarkUp/html3/forms.html
2. Another resource for forms information as well as general information about HTML is "John's HTML Tutor (indexed)," maintained by J. Alldred, available at:
   http://www.argonet.co.uk/users/protovale/tutor.html#form
3. An online book by SBT Accounting Systems contains a chapter about forms, "Chapter 7: HTML and Forms," available at:
   http://www.business1.com/int_book/ch07.htm
4. A tutorial about forms "The Form Element," can be found in the Web Developer's Virtual Library, available at:
   http://www.stars.com/Tutorial/HTML/Forms/

Module 7: Advanced HTML [II] Client-side imagemaps

Topics:

What is a client-side imagemap and why is it useful?
What are the basic components of imagemap markup?

Activities:

Create an imagemap that can be used as a table of contents for the resume

Resources:

IMAGEMAPS: Imagemaps provide an interesting way to link to other pages (or to other locations in the same page) because the different sections of a single image can be used to create different hypertext links. Here are five sites with information about imagemaps:

1. A useful introduction is "Geller's Guide to Incorporating Imagemaps into your HTML," available at:
   http://www.halcyon.com/davidg/imagemap.html
2. A useful resource is the "Welcome to the Imagemap Help Page - IhiP," maintained by S. Rogers, available at:
   http://www.hway.com/ihip/
3. Further discussion of "Client-side Imagemaps," also by S. Rogers, available at:
   http://www.hway.net/ihip/cside.html
4. A useful resource "Ithaca College ACCS Quick Guide: Imagemaps for the Web - A guide to making clickable imagemaps for World Wide Web pages," is maintained by C. Keller, available at:
   http://www.ithaca.edu/computing/quick_guides/imagemaps/imagemaps. html

A Training Template for Librarian-Trainers

As mentioned earlier in this chapter, training for librarians or staff members who will be training other library personnel and patrons mirrors the training programs described in the previous section. It also included a module which focuses on the training experience. For convenience, this module will be added on to the second program at the last session.

Module 8: Designing and running training sessions

Topics:

What are the critical success factors involved in effective Internet training programs?
How should training sessions be structured and run?
What are some useful strategies for delivering content and managing the interaction during the sessions?

Activities:

Present a 10-minute lecture on an Internet resource or service or on HTML markup
Lead an activity

Resources:

TRAINING: There are many sites on the Web that contain information of use to Internet trainers. Here are four sites with rich and useful information about training.:

1. The Library of Congress maintains a page of "Internet Guides, Tutorials, and Training Information," available at:
   http://lcweb.loc.gov/global/internet/training.html
2. A collection of links, the AICS "Top Ten" List of InterNet Training Resources" is available at:
   http://www.internet-hub.com/trainres.html
3. A similar collection is "ML's Training Page" maintained by M.L. Rice-Lively, available at:
   http://fiat.gslis.utexas.edu/~marylynn/mltrain.html
4. Another good source "Internet Training Resources" is available at:
   http://www.public.iastate.edu/~kushkows/itrain/itrain.html
5. Internet training materials are offered in "The SB204 Internet Teacher Training Project," maintained by UNR College of Education, University of Nevada, available at:
   http://unr.edu/homepage/sb204/

IS TRAINING WORTH THE TROUBLE?

Training is one of those activities that is easy to do poorly, which can lead to a range of problems for the organization, and worth doing well, because it can enhance the organization in many ways. Done correctly, training requires forethought and planning. Before becoming involved in the provision of training, whether for librarians and library staff, or for patrons, or both, librarians should take a hard and objective look at the costs and benefits of training programs for their organization. This chapter concludes with a discussion of the issues you should consider before you institute Internet training programs in your library. We begin with the issue of cost.

Training involves direct and indirect costs, both in terms of time and money. There is a commitment of time and energy that is necessary to prepare and deliver a series of training sessions. Even if the library decides to hire an outside consultant for initial sessions, the librarians who will be involved as trainers in subsequent sessions must be fully involved in these early sessions. There are indirect costs involved because they then must be able to expend the time to prepare and lead the sessions to follow; there are also costs involved in releasing librarians and staff from their duties to attend in-house training. If these sessions are held during working hours, librarian-trainers must be released from other responsibilities to lead them; if the sessions are held in the evenings, which is an option that caters to working patrons, other arrangements must be made—perhaps comp time or overtime pay; hence, direct costs.

For those who become involved in the provision of training, there are costs in terms of inconvenience and additional demands on their time which can affect their job performance. One outcome of establishing an informal role as a trainer in a library is that these people become seen by others in the organization as the main troubleshooters and consultants for computer and Internet problems. The flow of questions and requests can be disruptive for librarian-trainers and, as the problems increase in frequency and difficulty, can begin to monopolize their time, taking them way from their main job responsibilities. Providing post-training support for patrons can exacerbate this problem, especially considering that questions can come from walk-ins, e-mail, and by telephone.

Another problem is resistance to the adoption of the training role, from within the library and from the community. Librarians, administrators, or trustees may not think that the investment of time and money in the provision of training is worthwhile. They may argue that users, whether in-house or patrons, should learn what they need to do on their own and that the library's responsibility stops at the provision and maintenance of the hardware and software. There may be librarians and staff who refuse to learn how to use networked information resources and services or who resist the development of training programs for patrons. Resistance may also come from groups in the community, particularly local Internet service providers, who may be in the business of providing for-fee training and see any move by the library to provide training as direct competition.

A final problem arises out of the experience of introducing into any organization new information technologies, such as the hardware and software needed to set up and maintain an Internet connection. The librarian-trainer must stay current with the technologies which, in the realm of WWW browsers, requires considerable time and effort. Each new version of a browser includes modifications of existing features and the introduction of new features; after the trainer becomes familiar with the changes in the software, somehow users must be made aware of the changes in the tools they use. In addition, there are always unintended consequences that accompany the acquisition, installation, and maintenance of new technologies. Browsers can turn out to be more difficult to install and configure than expected, servers can be unstable, or there can be conflicts with other software running on the computer. Once users begin to put software through its paces, a range of problems will occur, many of which cannot be prepared for in advance.

Librarians thinking about implementing training programs have a number of options, all of which should be costed out to find the best fit for the organization's resources. The least expensive option is to do nothing. The hardware and software is put in place and the library's responsibility ends at the maintenance of their site. Although this option will use less of the library's financial resources, it also sets the stage for the underutilization of the library's Internet resources and a poor return on investment. A second option is to outsource the entire training process, which may be an expensive option. In addition, it leaves the library in a position of dependence. A third option is to outsource the sessions in which the librarians are trained who will eventually lead sessions with other library personnel and patrons. A fourth option is to outsource all of the in-house training and have librarian-trainers work with patrons. Finally, the library can handle the entire training program in-house.

Drawing these concerns together, the following is a list of issues that should be carefully considered when making decisions about the provision of training programs:

- What type of training will be offered?
- Who will conduct the training sessions?
- How many sessions will be used to train a typical staff member? patron?
- What content will be covered in each session?
- How many users will be trained at a time?
- What platforms will be used?
- What facilities will be used for training sessions?
- Will there be charges? If so, how much?

A set of benefits can accrue from involvement in Internet training. The creation of the trainer role can enhance the overall role of the librarian both within the library and in the community. The successful implementation of a training program can greatly improve the morale among librarians and staff as they acquire new and useful skills that they can employ in the conduct of their jobs.

The library can redefine its role in the community as an important information resource and service center by providing the Internet connection to patrons and helping them learn how to use it. The provision of training programs targeted at different patron users groups, such as parents and children, can enhance the standing of the library in the community. The training programs represent an exciting type of programming that can be used to draw many different patron groups into the library. Internet training is an effective form of outreach.

Successful training programs also represent an effective use of library resources because they will maximize the return on the investment made in hardware, software, and personnel. A successfully managed Internet WWW site will result in increases in use of the library's services and resources which can be quantified in walk-in traffic and "hits" on the site. Once the equipment is in place, librarians should have as a goal constant use of their Internet services and resources while the library is open.

Chapter 5

Looking to the Future: What's Next?

INTRODUCTION

Now that many libraries have taken their places on the Internet and librarians have begun to implement and manage increasingly sophisticated networked information resources and services, the secret can be told. Becoming a public digital library is akin to stepping onto a treadmill—a treadmill whose speed keeps increasing. There are changes that are occurring daily on the Internet, as new versions of Web browsers are released, new programs (plug-in and standalone) are made available for downloading, new generations of hardware and peripherals are brought to market, new programming languages are released (such as Java, Javascript, and Habanero), and new versions of HTML are approved by the World Wide Web Consortium. There are legislative, consensus-based, and software solutions that are being offered to the problem of regulating the Internet, such as the ill-fated *Communications Decency Act* (U.S.), the World Wide Web Consortium's *Platform for Internet Content Selection* (PICS), and filtering or blocking software.

It is no simple matter for librarians to keep up with these developments; many may find themselves running faster simply to stay in place! This last chapter explores future developments that may occur on and around the Internet and the potential impacts they may have for libraries. As with all prognostications, these speculations should be taken with the requisite grains of salt. The chapter concludes with some suggestions of ways that librarians can keep current with the rapidly changing world of digital networked information and resources that make up the Internet. Although these suggestions won't slow down the treadmill, they may allow us to catch our collective breath.

No one knows how large the Internet is—how many networks it links, how many host machines are on these networks, and how many people are using these machines. As a consequence, the estimates of the number of people on the Internet vary widely, but many observers seem convinced that at least 10 million and as many as 40 million people log onto the Internet on a regular basis. Many of these people are using their Internet connections for e-mail and Web browsing, and many of these connections are provided by commercial Internet service providers. Since 1988, the number of people on the Internet has been doubling each year, and, although this rate of increase cannot be maintained (the number of Net users would be larger than the population of the planet early in the next century), what is clear is that the Internet is becoming a mass-market and consumer phenomenon.

One trend worth noting is demographic. As the number of Internet users increases, the age of the average user will decrease and the mix of users will begin to resemble the composition of the general population. A survey of World Wide Web users done by the Georgia Institute of Technology has shown that the average user is likely to be a 33-year-old, upper-middle-class, educated, white male earning an average salary of almost $59,000 (U.S.). Over the next decade, many more families will obtain Internet accounts, taking advantage of the competition among commercial Internet services providers. Many more young people will come online as a consequence of their families' decisions to spend the equivalent each month of the monthly cable bill for a link to the Internet and their exposure to the Internet in schools. As researchers Bertot, McClure, and Zweizig express in a report for the National Commission on Libraries and Information Sciences, it is also clear that libraries, particularly public libraries, are riding the crest of this wave:

> At present, 44.6% of all public libraries have some type of Internet connection. This is an increase of 23.7% from the 20.9% level of public library connectivity in 1994 . . . Indeed, nearly all public libraries with population of legal service areas of 100,000 or greater have some type of Internet connection (percentage of connectivity ranging from 82.0% to 96.1%).

> When public libraries not currently connected to the Internet were asked to indicate future Internet connectivity plans, 56.7% indicated that their libraries planned to have some type of Internet connection by March 1997.

Meeker and DePuy, two analysts working for the Morgan Stanley Company, explain the growth potential of the Internet in different terms but come to similar conclusions. They estimate that there are currently 150 million personal computers users in the world, a number which they expect to reach 200 million by the turn of the century, which means that "the growth in Internet-connected computers will be strongly correlated with the rate of growth in the installed base of PCs." Most commentators agree that the convergence of computing and communications technologies is creating the conditions for the rapid growth of the networked digital information infrastructure for at least the next decade.

What is on the Internet horizon and how will it affect libraries? The next section considers some possible answers to that question.

LARGE SCALE CHANGES: WHAT'S COMING NEXT?

At a global level, there are socio-cultural, economic, and technological developments to which librarians should pay close attention. Socio-cultural changes involve the educational and community-building potential many see in the Internet, increased interest in the development of digital libraries, a trend toward regulating Internet content, and potential threats to privacy, security, and intellectual property posed by the increased flow of information across the Internet. Economic changes involve the rise of electronic commerce, as the Internet continues its transformation from a medium of information exchange to a medium for business, and the development of reliable and accurate charging mechanisms for Internet use. Technological changes involve continuing development of HTML, increasing sophistication and ease of use of Web browsing and peripheral software, the appearance of "push media," where content is delivered to the personal computer, and the convergence of telecommunications, networking, and broadcast media technologies.

This is by no means an exhaustive recounting of the ways in which the Internet may change over the next decade; these are merely some of the more obvious trends. In addition, the discussion which follows is clearly based on an optimistic view of the ways in which the Internet may change over time. There are commentators who present a much more pessimistic view of the future of the Internet, but we do not share these views. In addition, there is not sufficient space in this book to explore these changes in depth; instead, the discussion will sketch out the broad outlines of these developments.

Socio-Cultural Changes

The Internet will become a medium for education and community building. Since the beginning of the decade, Federal government agencies and advisory groups have stressed in a series of policy documents that there is a need to incorporate the Internet into American education and community life. For example, a 1996 report by the United States Advisory Council on the National Information Infrastructure (NII) outlines a set of "principles of education and lifelong learning" which depend, for their implementation, on the integration of the Internet into "electronic communities of learning." The Council states that "By the year 2000, all communities and all people should have convenient access to information and learning resources available through the [Internet] in their schools, colleges, universities, libraries, and other community-oriented institutions." They believe that the continued use of the Internet as a "tool to enhance education, training, and lifelong learning . . . will facilitate the reconstruction of our educational institutions and the redefinition of the roles of everyone involved with them—educators, administrators, librarians, parents, students, [and] employers . . . "

The Advisory Council has outlined specific initiatives to bring about these principles, including the following:

- stipulat[ing] that funds distributed via educational grant programs support projects that incorporate and/or facilitate access to and use of the [Internet] in K-12 schools, libraries, and community centers . . .
- creat[ing] incentives that encourage and enable the private sector to . . . play a larger role in making [Internet] resources available in schools, libraries, and community centers . . .
- chang[ing] the way teachers/librarians are educated so that the use of [Internet] technologies and resources is fully integrated into the initial training and certification process and the ongoing professional development of current teachers/ librarians . . . Requir[ing] that a portion of any government funds granted to support [Internet] educational projects are used to implement substantive, ongoing professional development programs for all educators/librarians who will be expected to utilize [Internet] technologies and resources.
- actively encourag[ing] business, governments, communities, and parents to create partnerships that will encourage/assist schools,

> libraries, and community centers to refocus their mission on becoming centers for lifelong learning and to use the [Internet] to facilitate their evolution.

For the past several years, commentators have emphasized the potential of the Internet as a teaching, instructional, and content-delivery tool in primary and secondary education. Many educators are experimenting with Internet-based curricula and resources, especially in the areas of science and social studies. For example, a number of ongoing collaborative efforts already link children in remote locations as they work on projects ranging from science experiments to collaborative writing. There are often messages on LISTSERV conferences populated by educators asking for e-mail penpals in other parts of the country or the world. There are online homework hotlines and experts who will answer e-mailed questions. There is a growing number of resources for educators in the arts and humanities as well. (For information on specific projects being used to introduce the Internet in education, see the Chapter Notes listing at the end of this book.)

The Internet also has a role in community building. According to the Morino Institute, the number of community networks and Freenets is increasing across the U.S., and they are becoming more of a presence in many communities. Steven E. Miller of Computer Professionals for Social Responsibility points out the importance of community building and argues that it must remain integral to the vision of the NII, which should involve a combination of:

> NII deployment with local organizational development. And not just any organizations, but specifically those that serve, advocate for, and are run by people from the parts of our society that are least likely to be able to buy their way into a market-driven NII that rations access according to personal income. In this context, people who are creating civic networks as a way of anchoring NII development in the needs and realities of local communities must go beyond making their facilities available to large numbers of individuals, even if those individuals are low-income, non-white, non-English speaking, or any of the other politically correct categories. We need to adopt a strategy of working through and with grassroots organizations.

A range of reasons are offered in support of the development of Internet-based community networks. They will strengthen the sense of community in a geographic region. Increased communication and information transfer among users will increase the sense of and participation in the community and serve as a medium which can be used at a grass-roots level to solve some of the problems facing the community. Community networks can be used to support economic growth, education, and social services and can ensure that the entire community, irrespective of income, is included in the evolving NII. They can help people develop computing and networking skills which will be crucial in an information economy, offer access to libraries and research institutions across the globe, and connect the citizenry to education institutions and other on-line resources. In a thesis on the Internet as part of community networks, A. Avis says that benefits can include the networking of "local non-profit organizations, improved delivery of social services," and the "provision of a central source of local information".

A key element in the development of Internet-based communities is access to e-mail, which seems to be the current contender for the status of "killer application." A report from the RAND Corporation recently concluded that "nearly universal access to e-mail within the United States could become feasible within a decade." Despite the fact that e-mail use is growing rapidly in certain sectors, many citizens, especially inner city and rural poor populations, are a long way from having easy access to the Internet. The RAND report states that most Americans will not have "access to e-mail well into the next century without societal intervention," and suggests that "universal e-mail might provide significant benefits in creating interactive communication among U.S. citizens and residents." The extension of e-mail capability throughout American society will create new channels of communication and information exchange among segments of the population that have been disenfranchised economically and politically. Universal e-mail, like universal telephone service, has the potential to spur new forms of political and social activism, especially if the service can be provided at low cost.

The interest in the development and implementation of digital libraries will increase as the major digital library projects near the end of their first funding cycle, according to the International Federation of Library Associations and Institutions. Taking place at six major research universities in the U.S., these projects have the potential to spin off a range of technologies that can be used to organize, manage, and provide access to large collections of digital information in a variety of forms, from text to still images, to full motion video. These projects, however, represent only the high end of the work going on in digital libraries, and it is not yet clear how they will affect public and school librarianship, where the funding necessary to take advantage of these high powered technologies is typically not available.

There is also a much larger grassroots effort which is under way and which will continue to occur involving the creation of public digital libraries. Many public and school libraries are mounting Web pages on their own or on commercial service providers' servers and are becoming information providers on the Internet. This is occurring without large-scale funding and without much fanfare. Librarians are finding themselves in the role of Web masters or mistresses in their organizations without a clear idea of the level of commitment and work that such a position entails and many times without any formal training. A small contribution of this book is to begin to clarify the ways in which the organization changes as Internet connections are implemented and raise the important issues that should be considered when deciding to step onto the digital treadmill.

As politicians become more aware of the uses of networked digital information, there will be increasingly strident attempts to regulate the flow of information on the global Internet across national boundaries. There will be an increasing number of more sophisticated legislative and legal initiatives to control both the content of Internet information and access to the Internet in the U.S. and in many other countries. The *Communications Decency Act* is the opening salvo in the battle to control the Internet in the U.S. Other nations, such as Singapore and China, have taken steps to define acceptable and unacceptable categories of networked digital information and to set sanctions for those who violate their regulations, whether by sending or receiving what is defined as pornographic materials or by criticizing the government. (For more detailed information, see the Chapter Notes at the end of the book.) The more public attention that is focused on the Internet, the more attempts there will be to regulate access to networked information, especially for children.

In addition to legislative attempts, there will also be consensus-based regulation, such as the World Wide Web Consortium's *Platform for Internet Content Selection*, described in Chapter 4. The logic seems to be that if Internet content providers take the initiative and engage in self labeling, then the political and legislative attempts at regulation can be forestalled. Along the same lines are the technological attempts at regulation, which involve the use of software designed to filter or block access to certain sites on the Internet; at the moment, many vendors are competing for market share on the basis of the extensiveness of their lists of blocked sites, the ease and frequency with which the software can be updated, and the difficulty of hacking the software.

At the same time, there will also be threats to intellectual property, privacy, and security. For example, the legal framework for managing copyright in a digital environment is in its early stages. Legal scholars and judges are examining the existing framework that has been used to handle print and non-networked non-print media (including software) and are attempting to determine which elements can be carried over into the digital networked environment and which must be changed. A recent report commissioned by the Executive Branch staked out an extreme position on the nature of digital copyright by claiming that when a Web page is displayed on a user's computer screen, copyright has been violated, since a copy of the page has been made in the computer's random access memory during the act of accessing and displaying it. What constitutes original digital information and what is a copy, and how the intellectual property of the creator of digital information can be protected and balanced against the fair use rights of the user in a networked digital environment will be the burning issues for the legal profession over the next decade.

There will be growing concern for the preservation of individual privacy in the digital networked environment. The ability to collect, store, organize, and provide access to databases of information about people is expanding as technologies improve. Already a number of search engines can be used to locate and find out information about people, and more Web servers are being configured to place files in users' hard drives (called *cookies*) which track the user's exploration of the site and which can be reexamined by the server the next time the user visits the site. This particular feature can be useful, because it streamlines the user's visit to the site and can allow a customized view of the site to be presented to the user. Although this form of "narrowcasting" represents an interesting trend, it also means that there is more information being collected about the individual, often without his or her consent, that can have value when sold to market researchers.

Cookies: Files stored on the user's hard drive which keep track of the way a particular Web site was explored.

The boundaries of individual privacy on the Internet are fluid and will become more so over time. Finally, as more sites appear, there will be increasing threats to security. More Internet users with Web pages and servers means more targets for those who break into systems. For example, a recent foray into the server of the Department of Justice in the late summer, 1996, resulted in an embarrassing display of profane language and sexually explicit images on the DOJ home page.

Economic Changes

One important economic change will be the rise of electronic commerce. One optimistic commentator, M.J. Cronin, predicts that the "Internet and other networks will totally redefine today's corporation within a few decades;" organizations will exhibit digital "teamwork, collaboration with business partners, and distributed decision making" and, wherever the customer is, the "company needs to find a way to be there too."

Currently, however, there are technical and cultural stumbling blocks to the growth of business on the Internet. Two critically important technical problems involve the development and implementation of scalable systems which can support transaction-based exchanges using some form of digital currency or credit and the ability to ensure the security and anonymity of these transactions to the satisfaction of the consumer. A third is the protection of sensitive and proprietary corporate information, an additional element which must be factored into an organization's decision to become involved in the digital networked environment. Work is proceeding on these problems and, when they are satisfactorily resolved, there will be a rush to market and electronic commerce will take off. For examples of projects that address these issues, see the Chapter References & Notes listing at the end of this book.

There will have to be a cultural change as well if electronic commerce is to succeed. Entrepreneurs must believe that there is a market among the millions of people who browse the Internet and that they can make a profit by selling to these people. They have to rethink their conceptions of marketing to encompass the unique features of the Internet marketplace; it is global, open 24 hours a day, and allows "narrowcasting," or marketing that can be targeted at specific niches of consumers.

Narrowcasting:
Marketing directed toward a specific group of consumers

Conceptions of advertising will have to change as business people realize that the rules of the marketing game have shifted; the point now is to bring potential consumers to their site and encourage them to explore. More of the purchasing decision will reside with the consumer. Net surfers have to become consumers who must come to believe that they can engage in the same type of secure exchanges on the Internet that they experience in the mall or, more appropriately, over the telephone when purchasing from mail order catalogs. Of course, consumers also have to believe that there are products of value to be had from Internet storefronts.

When this shift takes place, optimistic observers' predictions that 14 million buyers will rack up $24 billion in purchases by the year 2000 begin to sound believable. As D. Ruby comments in the Web document *The future of the net*, "once the public gains trust in secure online commerce, the Internet will truly have arrived as a mainstream shopping medium. Otherwise, it's just an interesting social experiment." There are signs that this change is beginning, as can be seen in a recent report by B. LeFurgy, stating that the two major commodities generating revenue for online businesses are computer components and books. Other types of electronic commerce that seem ready to explode are digital banking, electronic publishing, and Internet-based document delivery.

Technological Changes

There will be continual improvements in the technological infrastructure that supports the Internet; it will continue to expand and improve, becoming faster and more reliable over time. One important technological trend is interoperability, which means that as heterogeneous development of the Internet continues, there will be efforts made to ensure that incompatible systems and networks can seamlessly exchange data. As computer hardware and software companies build onto and maintain the Internet, telephone, cable television, entertainment, and publishing companies will compete to dominate the content and the means of its delivery over this infrastructure.

The standards that form the substructure of HTML will continue to undergo development, allowing for a more sophisticated presentation of Web-based information and services. According to a document prepared by Tim Berners-Lee, work is proceeding in the World Wide Web Consortium on specifications for a universal resource identifier that will describe a permanent address form for Web documents. Over the next few years, the competition will heat up between the major Web browser producers (especially Netscape and Microsoft) to define the *de facto* HTML standards in use, and the World Wide Web Consortium may find itself lagging behind the actual use of HTML as they struggle to set markup standards.

What this means for Web site developers is that they have to make decisions in their design process. They can take advantage of the new forms of markup and have a cutting edge site, but, in doing so, shut out potential visitors who may not be running the most current versions of the major browsers. They can also follow the approved HTML standards, allowing the greatest number of people to access their sites, but their sites will be less exciting.

Web browsers and peripheral software will become both more sophisticated and increasingly easier to use. Browsers will continue to evolve, incorporating more features that enhance the use of the Web, and, in all likelihood, will continue to be distributed as freeware with accelerating cycles of upgrading. The commercial software needed to develop and display advanced forms of multimedia will be available to developers and the shareware or freeware versions will be made available to users across the Web. The display of Web-based three dimensional imagery on a computer screen will be perfected; Web pages will begin to approach real time video in color, frame rate, and resolution. Text and image editors will become integrated into single pieces of software, such as can be seen in newer versions of Netscape Communicator Gold™, Microsoft Office™, Adobe PageMill™, and Corel WordPerfect™, making the design and creation of Web pages more intuitive; these will become valuable software packages for people who want to mark up their own pages. The cost of this software will drop over time, making Web design more accessible to non-technical users.

There are already products that are available for downloading that allow users with no programming experience to create and implement their own customized applications in the form of Java applets. One of the interesting potential consequences of these tools is that every user can be a publisher and producer of content, which means that the demand for two way interactivity and high bandwidth out of the user's home can be expected to increase.

One area of increasingly heated competition will be for the Internet dollars of the middle- and lower-middle-class user. Manufacturers are competing to produce low-end information appliances, such as WebTV™, which allows people to browse the Internet for several hundred dollars using devices that resemble television sets more than computers. The race is on to produce a device that is reliable, has sufficient display abilities and computing power to adequately render the range of data files that make up Web pages, and can be used easily by people with minimal computer training. Control of this market will make some company the Microsoft of the Web television! In addition, the speed of modems is increasing as the price is dropping; modem speeds of 48.800 bits per second and faster will soon be affordable to a broader market, allowing more people to take advantage of the full multimedia capabilities of the Web.

Among the interesting developments in new applications for the Web are tools that support interactivity. For example, one growth area is collaborative Web page authoring. Information exchange on the Web has been based on the hypertext link. People can easily create individual documents and link them, so that the whole becomes greater than the sum of the parts. This is certainly one model of cooperation, however, according to researchers Decouchant, Quint, and Salcedo, it is more interesting to move away from this traditional approach and consider "cooperative editing," where people can collaborate remotely on large, well-structured documents "writing a single document in a cooperative way."

Chatting: The ability to converse in real-time by exchanging typed information with participants in remote locations.

A second example of interactivity is "chatting," which is real-time interactive, text-based communication among people in remote locations. Internet Relay Chat (IRC) has been a telnet-based service that has a long history on the Internet, but recently, chat functionality has been incorporated into Web browsers and Web sites. The Internet Public Library (IPL) has taken this idea a step further than IRC by setting up the IPL MOO (Multi-User Object Oriented environment) as a site for interaction between net-patrons and IPL librarians. They see the MOO as:

> A place where a library community can form, where people can get together and interact in real time . . . One of the benefits of the moo is that interaction with other visitors and objects (desks, chairs, cat etc.) creates a mood conducive to virtual community. We have formed the framework where librarians and information seekers can gather together, talk, and provide reference services.
>
> This environment is text based and interactions are prefaced by simple commands. This is somewhat like sending text e-mail messages to a screenful of people and seeing everyone else's text responses at the same time. To give the process a real-life feel, the visitors are able to respond with emotions (in text) and interact with fellow visitors in a 'virtual building'. The Internet Public Library MOO is a specially created environment we are building to handle reference interviews and other collegial social gatherings.

LIBRARY RESPONSES

How will these developments impact libraries?

There will be increasing interest in expanding the educational and community-building potential of the Internet at all levels of education. Public and school libraries will come under increasing pressure to become involved in supporting the range of initiatives that are under way and are being planned. The relationships between the community networks and libraries have varied widely, with one extreme being competition between the two and the other being a merging of the two, meaning that involvement may take different forms, two of which are described later in this section. The library can become a hub for networked activities in the school and/or community. It can be a central location for access to networked information, with computers, modems, printers, and other peripherals in place. It can become a broadcast site as well, allowing users to produce and disseminate information they create. The library can also become an information producer in its own right, making portions of its collections available in digital form and creating new information products. In this way, the library can become an integral element of a community network, providing the facilities and environment within which the network can grow.

Another possibility is that the community network is based elsewhere and, although it will manage its own Internet site, the library takes on training and support functions. Librarians could offer a series of sessions for students and others in the community who wish to learn about the Internet. Regular Internet training classes are a useful way to increase the visibility of the library in the community. People can come into the library to learn about basic and advanced HTML markup, the use of Web browsers and the supporting software (plug-ins and standalone), the features of different search engines, the range of resources available on the Internet, and other information networking skills. If this response is chosen, librarians should be prepared to become involved in a continual process of monitoring the print and online information about Internet so that they can be maintaining and upgrading their networking skills. This will be necessary because the people who will seek out the assistance of librarians over Internet matters will also be ramping up their knowledge and abilities; their questions and requests will become more complex over time. Issues to be resolved involve the time and costs of providing such programming, but an argument can be made that this type of programming is as much within the library's purview as is a story hour for children or a resume writing workshop for adults.

Librarians should expect that there will be changes in the management structure and business processes within the library as a consequence of their development and implementation of an Internet site in the library. Maintaining a Web site in a library is a time- and labor-intensive activity that should not be done by people who can only devote "spare" time to the job. This means that job descriptions may have to be written, and new positions may have to be created. Aside from the technical issues involved in maintaining a site, there are a series of design and policy issues (discussed in Chapters 1, 2, and 3) which must be worked out. This can be most effectively done if librarians and staff agree in advance to undertake some type of participatory design process involving the major stakeholders in the effort and a formal process of policy development and evaluation.

In addition, librarians and staff will need to develop work routines which incorporate the maintenance and use of their Internet site's resources and services. Patrons will expect that the library has electronic resources as well as other resources that librarians will be able to access effectively for them. When they are able to access these resources and services through the library's Internet site, they will expect to see an organized approach to digital networked information resources and services provided by the library. Librarians will have to become involved in selecting and organizing the local digital information held by the library and providing an organized way to access Internet resources and services. This may require that librarians create online directories and resource guides to Internet information and make them accessible to patrons.

WHAT YOU CAN DO TO KEEP CURRENT

How will librarians keep up with the rapid development of the Internet and its miscellaneous resources if it continues to grow at the present rate? You can use a number of resources to keep abreast of the types of changes described in the previous section. Broadly speaking, there are three main categories of network-based sources of information you can access to find out what is happening on the net; there are World Wide Web sites, LISTSERV computer conferences, and USENET newsgroups that are outlets for the rapid dissemination of information about new software and hardware, changes in the laws and regulations covering Internet communications, and changes in the standards that support many Internet technologies and protocols.

These sources are recommended for two reasons. First, they tend to have more current information more quickly than will print resources, such as the trade magazines that cover the Internet. There are, for example, Web sites maintained by software and hardware manufacturers that will have press releases, bug fixes, announcements of new products, and other information well in advance of publications that are bound to print schedules. The second reason is that access to these sources, for the most part, is free. There are costs involved, such as the time required to read the e-mail from the LISTSERVs and to check in on the USENET newsgroups and Web sites, but this can become a routine part of people's work roles, if their responsibilities will include maintaining the library's Net presence.

What follows is not a comprehensive listing of sources, but a selective list that has proven to be useful to us over the years. As all good librarians do, you will look over this listing, select what seems useful, and use it as a springboard to develop your own set of sources. With listservs, the trick is to balance the number of lists to which one subscribes against the number of messages they produce, so that the daily load of e-mail messages is reasonable. With USENET newsgroups, a schedule can be developed so that one or two groups are checked each day, and, if a threaded newsreader is used, specific threads, or subject lines, can be followed. A bookmark list of useful Web sites is easy to create, and a similar schedule can be used to periodically check in with the sites that experience shows contain quality information. Another possibility for updating is to use and re-use a set of search terms on a series of search engines, to see when new information is put up onto the Web. Please note that all URLs in this section were working as of April 30, 1997. Also note that some of the annotations are taken from the home pages of these sites.

World Wide Web Sites

BrowserWatch

"Welcome to BrowserWatch, the leading site for information about browsers and plug-ins. We offer breaking news in the browser and plug-ins industry, as well as one of the most complete lists on development of different plug-ins and browsers. A quick check allows you to find the plug-ins or browsers you want quickly and effortlessly."

Available at http://browserwatch.iworld.com/

Coalition for Networked Information

"The Coalition for Networked Information was founded in March 1990 with a mission to help realize the promise of high performance networks and computers for the advancement of scholarship and the enrichment of intellectual productivity. The Coalition is a partnership of the Association of Research Libraries, CAUSE, and EDUCOM."

Available at http://www.cni.org/

Cool Tool of the Day

"What's a cool tool? Pretty much whatever we feel like. But, if you must have some sort of definition (you uptight thing you), it's any tool that makes your online life easier, more productive, more fun, stronger, faster, better . . . you name it. And we're not just countin' plug-ins either. Web development tools, Java toys, graphics thingies—we'll cover 'em all. Does that explain it? We hope so. Just keep coming back and you'll get the point."

Available at http://WWW.COOLTOOL.COM/maxanimation.html

EFF

"The Electronic Frontier Foundation is a non-profit civil liberties organization working in the public interest to protect privacy, free expression, and access to public resources and information online, as well as to promote responsibility in new media."

Available at http://www.eff.org

InterNIC

"In January of 1993 the InterNIC was established as a collaborative project between AT&T, General Atomics, and Network Solutions, Inc. NSI offers InterNIC Support Services and Net Scout Services. The InterNIC continues to participate in Internet forums and with the Research and Education community to promote Internet services, explore new tools and technologies, and to contribute to the rapidly growing Internet community."

Available at http://rs.internic.net/

Internet Resources Newsletter

"Internet Resources is a free WWW newsletter produced by Heriot-Watt University Library. It informs about new and recent Internet resources of interest to the higher education community. It also hopes to provide occasional guidance on various aspects of electronic information. It may be of use to anyone interested in the more serious aspects of the Internet and its resources."

Available at http://www.hw.ac.uk/libWWW/irn/irn.html

Internet Society

"The Internet Society is the international organization for global cooperation and coordination for the Internet and its Internet working technologies and applications. Its members reflect the breadth of the entire Internet community and consist of individuals, corporations, non-profit organizations, and government agencies. Its principal purpose is to maintain and extend the development and availability of the Internet and its associated technologies and applications—both as an end in itself, and as a means of enabling organizations, professions, and individuals worldwide to more effectively collaborate, cooperate, and innovate in their respective fields and interests."

Available at http://info.isoc.org/

Microsoft Site Builder network

"The Site Builder Network is a new program from Microsoft that supports the efforts of Web developers and designers to create interactive, revenue-generating, traffic-building, and just plain beautiful Web sites. It's your one-stop, direct link to a wealth of technical information, products, technologies, and support from Microsoft and other leaders in Web technology, such as Adobe and Macromedia."

Available at http://www.microsoft.com/sitebuilder

Netscape

"Aside from the general news of the range of products that is available, there is a Technical Support area where you can find a wealth of helpful information about your Netscape software and how to overcome any problems you might encounter with it, either on your own or with the help of our technical support team."

Available at http://home.netscape.com/

Net Scout

"Net Scout Services researches Internet resources and network tools and reports the findings back to the community. Our primary goal is to provide valuable information to educators and researchers in the U.S. about using the Internet effectively. However, everyone is welcome to use the publications and Web sites provided by Scout Services, and we encourage feedback and suggestions from the entire Internet community."

Available at http://rs.internic.net/scout/report/

News.com

"News.Com is the first online, free, up-to-the-minute news source devoted entirely to technology. If you need to know what's happening in computing, on the Net, and in technology business, News.Com is what you need. Updated as news occurs throughout the day, News.Com is presented using the absolute latest Internet multimedia technologies."

Available at http://www.news.com/

Sun Microsystems

"A source for information about hardware and software produced by Sun Microsystems."

Available at http://www.sun.com/

SunWorld Online

"An electronic magazine which is not affiliated with Sun Microsystems. It covers events and products that affect how you use SPARC and Solaris machines and products created for them by Sun and other vendors. There is also information about the technology behind Unix-based, client/server technologies, Java, and other networking technologies."

Available at http://www.sun.com/sunworldonline/

W3 Consortium's Platform for Internet Content Selection

"PICS is an infrastructure for associating labels with Internet content. It was originally designed to help parents and teachers control what children access on the Internet, but it also facilitates other uses for labels, including code signing, privacy, and intellectual property rights management."

Available at http://www.w3.org/pub/WWW/PICS/

Computer Conferences

Discussion of Netscape <netscape@danann.hea.ie>

To subscribe, send a message:

subscribe netscape First name Last name

to:

listserv@listserv.hea.ie

Edupage <educom@educom.unc.edu>

"Edupage, a summary of news about information technology, is provided three times a week as a service by Educom, a Washington, D.C.-based consortium of leading colleges and universities seeking to transform education through the use of information technology."

To subscribe, send this message

subscribe edupage Firstname Lastname

to:

listproc@educom.unc.edu

EFFector Online <editors@eff.org>

"A publication of the Electronic Frontier Foundation, a non-profit civil liberties organization working in the public interest to protect privacy, free expression, and access to public resources and information online, as well as to promote responsibility in new media."

To subscribe, send message
subscribe effector-online
to:
listserv@eff.org

Back issues are available at:
ftp.eff.org, /pub/EFF/Newsletters/EFFector/
gopher.eff.org, 1/EFF/Newsletters/EFFector
http://www.eff.org/pub/EFF/Newsletters/EFFector/

Internet Scout Report

A weekly review of new and noteworthy Internet resources, sponsored by InterNIC.

To subscribe send a message:
subscribe SCOUT-REPORT First Name Last name
to:
listserv@lists.internic.net

Net-happenings <net-happenings@lists.internic.iet>

To subscribe, send the command:
subscribe net-happenings Your Name
to:
listserv@lists.internic.net

Seidman's Online Insider

A weekly summary of major online services and Internet events.

To subscribe, send an e-mail message
subscribe online-l firstname lastname
to:
listserv@peach.Ease.Lsoft.Com

A Web-based version of the newsletter is available at http://www.netguidemag.com.

Web4Lib <web4lib@library.berkeley.edu>

"The Web4Lib electronic discussion exists to foster discussion of issues relating to the creation and management of library-based World-Wide Web servers and clients. Particularly appropriate issues for discussion include, but are not limited to, Web resource selection and information mounting in relation to existing acquisition and collection development procedures; cataloging issues regarding Web information; and in-house patron access to Web servers (for example, Mosaic on patron-accessible computers)."

To subscribe, send the message
subscribe Web4Lib your name
to:
listserv@library.berkeley.edu

Archives available at http://sunsite.berkeley.edu/Web4Lib/

USENET Newsgroups

comp.infosystems.www.authoring.html
comp.infosystems.www.authoring.images
comp.infosystems.www.authoring.misc
comp.infosystems.www.browsers.mac
comp.infosystems.www.browsers.misc
comp.infosystems.www.browsers.windows
comp.infosystems.www.servers.mac
comp.infosystems.www.servers.misc
comp.infosystems.www.servers.sun
comp.infosystems.www.servers.windows
comp.internet.library
comp.internet.net-happenings
comp.org.cpsr.announce
comp.org.cpsr.talk
comp.org.eff.news
comp.org.eff.talk
comp.org.isoc.interest
comp.www.browsers

Chapter References & Notes

INTRODUCTION

Bertot, John Carlo; Charles R. McClure, and Douglas L. Zweizig. 1996. *The 1996 National Survey of Public Libraries and the Internet: Progress and Issues: Final Report.*
Available at: http://istweb.syr.edu/Project/Faculty/McClure-NSPL96/NSPL96_3.html

Cailliau, Robert. 3 October 1995. *A Little History of the World Wide Web.*
Available at: http://www.w3.org/pub/WWW/History.html

Civille, Richard. 1995. The Internet and the Poor. In B. Kahin and J. Jeller (Eds.), *Public Access to the Internet*. Cambridge, MA: MIT Press, pp. 175-207.
Available at:gopher://nic.merit.edu:7043/00/conference.proceedings/harvard.pubaccess.symposium/network.communities/internet-poor.txt

CyberAtlas. 1996. *CyberAtlas Market Size.*
Available at: http://www.cyberatlas.com/market.html (and)

Gray, Matthew. 1996. *Web Growth Summary*.
Available at: http://www.mit.edu:8001/people/mkgray/net/web-growth-summary.html

Henderson, Carol C., and Frederick King. 1995. The Role of Public Libraries In Providing Public Access to the Internet. In B. Kahin

and J. Jeller (Eds.), *Public Access to the Internet*. Cambridge, MA: MIT Press, p. 157.
See also: http://www.nlc-bnc.ca/ifla/documents/libraries/net/publib.txt

Information Revolution and the Public Library.
Available at: http://www.lff.org/technology/basics.html

Internet Society Press Release. 2 August 1995. *Internet Survey Reaches 6.6 Million Internet Host Level:First Half 1995 Growth Is 37 Percent*.
Available at: http://info.isoc.org:80/infosvc/press/020895press.txt

Markoff, John. 8 December 1993. A Free and Simple Computer Link. *New York Times*, p. D1.

McClure, Charles. March/April 1995. Public Access to the Information Superhighway through the Nation's Libraries. *Public Libraries*, pp. 81-82.

Microsoft Corporation. 1997. *Download Area*.
Available at: http://www.microsoft.com/ie/download/
"You're just a few steps away from downloading Internet Explorer and choosing from an array of add-on products that let you get more out of the Web."

Netcraft. 1997. *The Netcraft Web Server Survey*.
Available at: http://www.netcraft.com/survey/

Netscape Communications Corporation. 1996. *Download Netscape Software*.
Available at: http://home.netscape.com/comprod/mirror/index.html
"If you are a student, staff member, or faculty member of an educational institution, charitable nonprofit organization, or public library, you may download Netscape Navigator and Netscape Servers for free. All Netscape products that are available for electronic download are free to educational institutions, charitable nonprofit organizations, and public libraries."

Netscape Communications News Release. 13 October 1994. *Netscape Communications Offers New Network Navigator Free on the Internet*.
Available at: http://home.netscape.com/newsref/pr/newsrelease1.html

Network Wizards. No date. *Number of Internet Hosts*.
Available at: http://www.nw.com/zone/host-count-history

Network Wizards. 1997. *Internet Domain Survey, January 1997.*
Available at: http://www.nw.com/zone/WWW/report.html (and)

Domain Survey Notes.
Available at: http://www.nw.com/zone/WWW/notes.html

Nua Ltd. 17 December 1996. *Internet Survey Companies And Consultancies.*
Available at: http://www.nua.ie/surveys/companies.html

Sackman, Gleason. 1 March 1997. *Hotlist of K-12 School Internet Sites—Cumulative Totals—USA*
Available at: http://rrnet.com/~gleason/totalsta.htm

U.S. Department of Commerce. July 1995. *Falling Through The Net.*
Available at: http://www.ntia.doc.gov/ntiahome/fallingthru.html

U.S. Department of Education. Office of Educational Research and Improvement. February 1996. *Advanced Telecommunications in U.S. Public Elementary and Secondary Schools, 1995*, p.3.

Zakon, Robert Hobbes. 1993; 15 August 1996. *Hobbes' Internet Timeline v2.5*
Available at: http://info.isoc.org/guest/zakon/Internet/History/HIT.html

See also the following books for more information on connecting to the Internet:

Estrada, Susan. 1993. *Connecting to the Internet*. Sebastopol, CA: O'Reilly & Associates, Inc.

Krol, Ed. 1994. *The Whole Internet User's Guide & Catalog*. Sebastopol, CA: O'Reilly & Associates.

Schneider, Karen G. 1996. *A Librarian's Commonsense Guide to Low-cost Connections*. New York, NY: Neal-Schuman Publishers.

CHAPTER ONE

Bertot, John Carlo; Charles R. McClure and Douglas L. Zweizig. *The 1996 National Survey of Public Libraries and the Internet: Progress and Issues: Final Report.*
Available at: http://istweb.syr.edu/Project/Faculty/McClure-NSPL96/NSPL96_3.html

Connolly, Dan and Dave Raggett; World Wide Web Consortium. (No date). *Introducing HTML 3.2.*
Available at: http://www.w3.org/pub/WWW/MarkUp/Wilbur/

Gillespie, Thom and Karla Alexander, Candice Bertotti, Dung-lan Chen, Sheau-hui Ching, Norico Hara, Huey-ying Hsu, Chris Jackson, Tim Jones, Rosemary Lovely, Brett Pfingston. 19 December 1995. *The Public Web Project: Raw Research Regarding Designing a Web Site for the Monroe County Public Library Version*
Available at: http://www.indiana.edu/~slizzard/pwp/pwp.html

HTML Editorial Review Board; World Wide Web Consortium. *The Structure of HTML 3.2 Documents*
Available at: http://www.w3.org/pub/WWW/MarkUp/Wilbur/features.html

Horton, William. 1994. *The Icon Book: Visual Symbols for Computer Systems and Documentation.* New York, NY: John Wiley and Sons, Inc., p. 29.

Jackson, Christopher. 30 October 1996. *Public Web Project.* E-mail to L. Champelli (lchampel@indiana.edu).

Johnson, Roberta. 18 March 1996. *Dewey on the Web.* E-mail to L. Champelli (lchampel@indiana.edu).

King, Andrew B. May 1995; 2 December 1996. *What Makes a Great Web Site?*
Available at: http://webreference.com/greatsite.html

Leita, Carole. 12 March 1996. Telephone interview with L. Champelli.

Loosmorre, Judy. November/December 1994.. Color in Instructional Communication. *Performance and Instruction*, pp. 33, 36-38.

Morton Grove Public Library. 1995; 27 November 1996. *About the MGPL Web Site.*
Available at: http://www.nslsilus.org/mgkhome/mgpl/aboutwww.html

Morton Grove Public Library. 1995; 13 May 1996. *MGPL Collection Development & Materials Selection Policy - World Wide Web Sites*
Available at: http://www.nslsilus.org/mgkhome/colldev/adultmis.html#WWW

Morton Grove Public Library. 30 December 1996. *Morton Grove Public Library*
Available at: http://www.nslsilus.org/mgkhome/

Provo City (Utah) Public Library. *Provo City Library.*
Available at: http://www.provo.lib.ut.us/

Public Web Project.
Available at: http://www.indiana.edu/~slizzard/pwp/pwp.html

Rosenfeld, Louis B. Winter 1994. Guides, Clearinghouses and Value-Added Repackaging: Some Thoughts on How Librarians Can Improve the Internet. *Reference Service Review*, 22, 11-16.

Sano, Darrell. 1996. *Designing Large-Scale Web Sites: A Visual Desgin Methodology.* New York: Netscape Communications Corporation. John Wiley and Sons, Inc., p. 9.

Shafer, Keith. 27 December 1996. *A Brief Introduction to Scorpion.*
Available at: http://orc.rsch.oclc.org:6109/bintro.html

University of California. *INFOMINE: Scholarly Internet Resource Collections.*
Available at: http://lib-www.ucr.edu/infomine/exp/intro.html

To find other libraries on the Web, see one of the following lists:

Bertland, Linda. 12 December 1996. *School Libraries on the Web: A Directory.*
Available at: http://www.voicenet.com/~bertland/libs.html

Collins, Stephen. *Web66 International WWW Schools Registry.*
Available at: http://web66.coled.umn.edu/schools.html

Dowling, Thomas. 1995; 1996; 2 January 1997. *Libweb: Library Servers via WWW.*
Available at: http://sunsite.berkeley.edu/Libweb/

Milbury, Peter. 26 September 1996. *Peter Milbury's School Library & School Librarian Web Pages*
Available at: http://www.cusd.chico.k12.ca.us/~pmilbury/lib.html

Milton Public Library. 1 January 1997. *Public Libraries on the WWW.*
Available at: http://www.tiac.net/users/mpl/public.libraries.html

Milton (MA) Public Library (http://www.tiac.net/users/mpl/) has also compiled and annotated a list of public libraries with Web sites. It also includes design guidelines for public libraries.
Available at: http://www.tiac.net/users/mpl/guidelines.html

Napoli, Don; Saint Joseph County Public Library. 1995; 29 February 1996. *SJCPL's List of Public Libraries with Internet Services.*
Available at: http://sjcpl.lib.in.us/homepage/PublicLibraries/PublicLibraryServers.html

Persons, Patrick. *Public Library Youth Department Web Pages in the United States.*

Available at: http://metronet.lib.mi.us/CANT/ypages.html

Sackman, Gleason. 1994; 2 January 1997. *HotList of K-12 Internet School Sites.*
Available at: http://rrnet.com/~gleason/k12.html

TriPath Network—a project of the Three Rivers and Pathfinders library systems. *Cool Library Site of the Week.*
Available at: http://www.colosys.net/coolib/

Additional sources for learning more about HTML and Web design:

Berkeley Digital Library Sunsite. 5 December 1996. *Guidelines for Web Document Style & Design*
Available at: http://sunsite.berkeley.edu/Web/guidelines.html

Berners-Lee, Tim; World Wide Web Consortium. 1995. *Style Guide for online hypertext.*
Available at: http://www.w3.org/pub/WWW/Provider/Style/Overview.html

Castro, Elizabeth. 1997. *HTML for the World Wide Web*, 2nd Edition. Berkeley, CA: Peachpit Press.

Heinich, Robert. 1996. *Instructional Media and Technologies for Learning*, 5th Edition. New Jersey: Prentice-Hall, Inc.

Levine, Rick; Sun Microsystems. 1995; 2 August 1996. *Guide to Web Style.*
Available at: http://www.sun.com/styleguide/tables/Welcome.html

Lemay, Laura. 1996. *Teach Yourself Web Publishing with HTML 3.0 in a Week*. Indianapolis, IN: Sams.net Publishing.

Nielsen, Jakob; Sun Microsystems. May 1996. *Top Ten Mistakes in Web Design.*
Available at: http://www.useit.com/alertbox/9605.html
Also at: http://www.sun.com/960416/columns/alertbox/index.html

Savola, Tom. 1995. *Using HTML.* Indianapolis, IN: Que.

Tufte, Edward R. 1990. *Envisioning Information*. CT: Graphics Press.

CHAPTER TWO

Research institutions receiving NSF funding for digital library projects:

Six research institutions received multi-year NSF funding for high end digital library projects. The work is in its early stages and is fairly technical, with few indications of easy applications to the world of public and school libraries. Such developments will eventually filter down, but not in the near future. The institutions are listed here along with URLs that link to their project pages:

Informedia. 1996. *The Informedia™ Digital Video Library Project.* Carnegie Mellon University.
Available at: http://fuzine.mt.cs.cmu.edu/im/

Stanford University. 1996. *Stanford University Digital Libraries Project.*
Available at: http://diglib.stanford.edu/diglib/

University of California at Berkeley. 1996. *UC Berkeley Digital Library Project.*
Available at: <http://elib.cs.berkeley.edu/>

University of California at Santa Barbara. 1996. *Alexandria Digital Library Project.*
Available at: <http://alexandria.sdc.ucsb.edu/>

University of Illinois at Urbana-Champaign. 1996. *Digital Library Initiative: Federating Repositories of Scientific Literature.*
Available at: <http://www.grainger.uiuc.edu/dli/>

University of Michigan, Ann Arbor, Michigan. 1996. *The University of Michigan Digital Library Project.*
Available at: http://www.sils.umich.edu/UMDL/HomePage.html

Chapter References:

Abrahams, J., J. Clement, and M. Parris. 1995. A list of schools in the United States with high-bandwidth connectivity to the Internet.
Available at: http://k12.cnidr.org/janice_k12/states/current_march.html

American Civil Liberties Union; Human Rights Watch; Electronic Privacy Information Center; Electronic Frontier Foundation; Journalism Education Association; Computer Professionals for Social Responsibility; National Writers Union; Clarinet Communications Corp.; Institute for Global Commu-

nications; Stop Prisoner Rape; Aids Education Global Information System; Bibliobytes; Queer Resources Directory; Critical Path Aids Project, Inc.; Wildcat Press, Inc.; Declan Mccullagh dba Justice on Campus; Brock Meeks dba Cyberwire Dispatch; John Troyer dba The Safer Sex Page; Jonathan Wallace dba The Ethical Spectacle; and Planned Parenthood Federation Of America, Inc., Plaintiffs, v. Janet Reno, in her official capacity as Attorney General Of The United States, United States District Court

Eastern District Of Pennsylvania. Civ. No. 96-963. (1996). Available at: http://www.epic.org/free_speech/censorship/lawsuit/complaint.html>

American Library Association. Office of Intellectual Freedom. 1995. *Intellectual Freedom Manual*, 5th Edition. Chicago, IL: ALA.

American Library Association. Office of Intellectual Freedom. 1996. *Access to Electronic Information, Services, and Networks: an Interpretation of the Library Bill Of Rights.* Available at: gopher://ala1.ala.org:70/00/alagophx/alagophxfreedom/electacc.fin

Cavazos, E.A. and G. Morin. 1995. *Cyberspace and the Law: Your Rights and Duties in the On-line World*. Cambridge, MA: The MIT Press, pp. 67, 70.

Champelli, L. 1996. *The Internet Advocate: A Web-based Resource Guide for Librarians and Educators Interested in Providing Youth Access to the Net.* Available at: http://www.monroe.lib.in.us/~lchampel/netadv.html

Georgia State Legislature. 1996. *HB 1630 Computer or telephone network; transmitting misleading data*.
Available at: http://www.ganet.state.ga.us/cgi-bin/pub/leg/legdoc?billname'1995 / HB1630&docpart=full&highlight=HB_1630
If this site moves again, go to the Legislative Services page <http://www.ganet.state.ga.us/services/ >. At the bottom of the page (which is the right-hand frame) select the **1995-1996** legislative session and click on **View Session**. Then try searching the term *HB 1630*.

Gray, M. 1996. *Measuring the Growth of the Web: June 1993 to June 1995.* Available at http://www.mit.edu:8001/people/mkgray/growth/

Hoffman, D.L, W. D. Kalsbeek, and T. P. Novak. 1996. *Internet Use in the United States: 1995 Baseline Estimates and Preliminary Market Segments*.
Available at: http://www2000.ogsm.vanderbilt.edu/baseline/1995.Internet.estimates.html

Ingram, Catherine E. 1996. *A Public Librarian's Guide to Internet Access*.
Available at: http://recall. lib.indiana.edu/~caingram/IF/index.html

Internet Public Library. 1996.
Available at: http://ipl.sils.umich.edu/
The MOO at the Internet Public Library <http://www.ipl.org/moo/> is explained as follows: "A *MOO* is a Multi-User Object Oriented environment, an interactive system accessible through telnet by many users at the same time. Moos are based on the MUD (Multi-User Dungeon) concept, but include more possibilities for interaction and real time communication learning experiences.

Why telnet to the MOO?
The Internet Public Library is a place where a library community can form, where people can get together and interact in real time. In this environment the community can help shape their surroundings and make it a place that fits their needs. One of the benefits of the moo is that interaction with other visitors and objects (desks, chairs, cat etc.) creates a mood conducive to virtual community. We have formed the framework where librarians and information seekers can gather together, talk, and provide reference services."

Internet Public Library. 1996. *Server Access Log Policy*.
Available at: http://www.ipl.org/about/circpol.html

Kinneman, D. 1996. *Critiquing Acceptable Use Policies*.
Available at: http://www.io.com/~kinnaman/aupessay.html

Krug, J.F. 1996. Preface. In Office for Intellectual Freedom. *Intellectual Freedom Manual*, 5th Edition. Chicago. IL: American Library Association. x.

Libraries for the Future. 1996. *Local Places, Global Connections: Models of Public Library Connectivity*.
Available at: http://www.lff.org/technology/local.html

McClure, C.R., W. C. Babcock, K. A. Nelson, J. A. Polly, and S. R. Kankus. 1994. *The Project GAIN Report: Connecting Rural Public Libraries to the Internet*. Liverpool, NY: Nysernet.

National Research Council. Commission on Physical Sciences, Mathematics, and Applications. Computer Science and Telecommunications Board. NRENAISSANCE Committee. 1994. *Realizing the Information Future: The Internet and Beyond.* Washington, D.C.: National Academy Press.

National Research Council. 1994. Rights and Responsibilities of Participants in Networked Communities. Washington, D.C.: National Academy Press.
Available at: http://www.nap.edu/readingroom/books/rights/

Resnick, P. and M. Hill. 1996. *PICS: Internet Access Controls Without Censorship.*
Available at: http://www.w3.org/pub/WWW/PICS/iacwc.htm

Sackman, Gleason. 1995. HotList of K-12 Internet School Sites—USA—1 November 1995.
Available at: http://rrnet.com/~gleason/k12.html

Saint Joseph County Public Library. 1996. *SJCPL's List of Public Libraries with Internet Services.*
Available at: http://sjcpl.lib.in.us/homepage/PublicLibraries/PublicLibraryServers.html

United States Congress. 1996. *Telecommunications Act of 1996.*
Available at: http://www.technologylaw.com/techlaw/telecom_bill.html
See also Appendix A.

United States National Information Infrastructure Advisory Council. 1995. *KickStart Initiatives: Connecting America's Communities to the Information Superhighway.*
Available at: http://www.benton.org/Library/KickStart/kick.privacyresources.html

United States National Information Infrastructure Advisory Council. 1995.
Available at: http://www.benton.org/Library/KickStart/kick.intellectualproperty.html #question1

United States Department of Commerce. National Telecommunications and Information Administration. Office of Telecommunications and Information Applications. 1995.

W3 Consortium. 1996. *Platform for Internet Content Selection.*
Available at: http://www.w3.org/pub/WWW/PICS/

The White House. 1996. *A Short Summary of the Telecommunications Reform Act of 1996.*
Available at http://www2.whitehouse.gov/WH/EOP/OP/telecom/summary.html

CHAPTER THREE

American Library Association. Office of Intellectual Freedom. *(Draft Version 1.1) Questions and Answers about Access to Electronic Information, Services and Networks.*
Available at: gopher://ala1.ala.org:70/00/alagophx/alagophxfreedom/electacc.q%26a

———, 24 January 1996. *Access to Electronic Information, Services, and Networks: An Interpretation of the LIBRARY BILL OF RIGHTS*
Available at: gopher://ala1.ala.org:70/00/alagophx/alagophxfreedom/electacc.fin

Broyles, Linda. 12 April 1996. *Permission to Reprint SJCPL Comp.Use Policy.* E-mail to L. Champelli (lchampel@indiana.edu).

———, 9 October 1996. *SJCPL Comp. Use/Internet Policy.* E-mail to L. Champelli (lchampel@indiana.edu).

Buchanan, Nancy. 10 April 1996. *UH Libraries Web.* E-mail to L. Champelli (lchampel@indiana.edu)

Burger, Robert. Summer 1986. The Analysis of Information Policy. *Library Trends, 35,* p. 173.

Canby, Oregon, Public Library. *Canby, Oregon, Public Library Internet Access Policy.*
Available at: http://www.ci.oswego.or.us/library/canby.htm

Cisler, Steve. 1993. *Protection and the Internet.*
Available at: ftp://ftp.apple.com/alug/rights/internet.protection
(and)
Available at: http://caviar.mic.ucla.edu/internet-protection.html

Durrant, M. Guy. 19 February 1996. *State Internet AUP?* E-mail to L. Champelli (lchampel@indiana.edu).

Emory University. October 1994; March 1, 1996. *Information Technology Use Policy.*
Available at: http://www.cc.emory.edu/ITD/POLICY/intro.html

Flanders, Bruce. 5 March 1996. *Internet Problems.* PUBLIB-NET LISTSERVE.
Formerly: gopher://nysernet.org:70/0R0-2669-/Special%20Collections%3A%20Libraries/ Publib%20Archive/1995/960305
For information on retrieving, see:
http://sunsite.berkeley.edu/PUBLIB/archive.html

Florida International University. 7 April 1995. *Florida International University—World Wide Web Policies.*
Available at: http://www.fiu.edu/webpolicy.html

Funk, Evie. 18 March 1996. *Your Internet Use Policy.* E-mail to L. Champelli (lchampel@indiana.edu).

Hill, Charles. 17 March 1996. *AUP Message.* E-mail to L. Champelli (lchampel@indiana.edu).

Huffman, Mike. 14 February 1996. *Internet Use Policy.* E-mail to L. Champelli (lchampel@indiana.edu)

JONESL2. 20 January 1996. *Supervision of students on Internet.* LM_NET School Media Specialists Listserv.
Available at: gopher://ericir.syr.edu:70/0R2349528-2349923-/Listservs/LM_NET/1996/ Jan_1996

Justie, Kevin. 9April 1996. *MGPL Internet Access Policy / 'Pre-Home pages'.* E-mail to L. Champelli (lchampel@indiana.edu).

Lawrence Public Library Board of Trustees. 15 May 1995; 25 April 1996. *Lawrence Public Library Internet Access Guidelines.*
Available at: http://www.idir.net/~lpl/iag.html

Leita, Carole. 11 November 1996. *Berkeley Public Library Internet Use Policy.*
Available at: http://www.ci.berkeley.ca.us/bpl/files usepolicy.html

Manning, B. and D. Perkins. *Internet School Networking Group. Internet Draft: Acceptable Use Policy Definition*
Available at: gopher://riceinfo.rice.edu:1170/00/More/Acceptable/bmanning

Mapes, Bruce and Nina Stull. 25 September 1995. *Newark Memorial High School Library. Welcome to the Internet.*
Available at: http://www.infolane.com/nm-library/m_page.html

McDonald, Fran. 18 August 1994. *Minnesota Coalition Against Censorship Internet Statement.*
Available at: gopher://riceinfo.rice.edu:1170/00/More/Acceptable/minnaup

McKenzie, Jamie. 20 February 1996. *Bellingham Network Policy.* E-mail to L. Champelli. (lchampel@indiana.edu).

———, May 1995. Creating Board Policies for Student Use of the Internet. In *From Now On, 5*, pg. 7.
Available at: http://www.pacificrim.net/~mckenzie/fnomay95.html

Morton Grove Public Library Board of Trustees. 12 October 1995. *Internet Access Policy.*
Available at: http://www.nslsilus.org/mgkhome/mgpl/mgplpol.html#internet

———, *The Internet at the Morton Grove Public Library.*
Available at: http://www.nslsilus.org/mgkhome/mgpl/prehome.html

National Science Foundation. February 1992. *NSFnet Backbone Services Acceptable Use Policy.*
Available at: gopher://riceinfo.rice.edu:1170/00/More/Acceptable/nets/nsfnet.txt

Office for Intellectual Freedom. 1992. Free Access to Libraries for Minors. In *Intellectual Freedom Manual,* 4th Edition. Chicago, IL: American Library Association., p. 17.
Available at: gopher://gopher.eff.org:70/00/CAF/library/access.minors.ala

Putnam Valley School District. *Putnam Valley Computer Use Policy.*
Available at: http://putwest.boces.org/PVTech/Use.html

Rau, Anne. 10 February 1996. *Why Writing AUPs?* E-mail to L. Champelli (lchampel@indiana.edu).
Note: Rau's message was sent in response to Feb 9 posting from L. Champelli to the publib-net listserv
Formerly: gopher://nysernet.org:70/0R12527-14460-/Special%20Collections%3A% 20Libraries/Publib%20Archive/1995/960209
For information on retrieving, see: http://sunsite.berkeley.edu/PUBLIB/archive.html

Rezmierski, Virginia. March/April 1995. Computers, Pornography, and Conflicting Rights. In *Educom Review.* 30(2).
Available at: gopher://ivory.educom.edu/00/educom.review/review.95/mar.apr/rezmier

Rose, Lance. 1995. *Netlaw. Your Rights in the Online World.* Berkeley, CA: Osborne McGraw Hill, pg. 39.

Saint Joseph County Public Library Board. 1995; 23 September 1996. *St. Joseph County Public Library Computer Usage Policy and Disclaimer.*
Available at: http://sjcpl.lib.in.us/homepage/Reference/ComputUsePolicy.html

Salem, Oregon/Salem Public Library. 14 October 1996. *OPEN Internet Access Policy.*
Available at: http://www.open.org/library/internet.html

Southeastern Universities Research Association. May 1994. *SURAnet Acceptable Use Policy.*
Available at: http://jhuniverse.hcf.jhu.edu/www/jhuniv/suranet.html

Stull, Nina. 20 March 1996. *Internet Use.* E-mail to L. Champelli (lchampel@indiana.edu).

Whitmill, Glenna. 22 July 1996. Telephone interview with L. Champelli.

Willard, Nancy. 1996. *A Legal and Educational Analysis of K-12 Internet Acceptable Use Policies.*
Available at: http://www.erehwon.com/k12aup/legal_analysis.html

Williams College. *Policies, Rules, Laws, Principles, Aphorisms.*
Available at: http://www.williams.edu/Policies/

Yale University. January 1996; 29 July 1996. *Institutional WWW Account Information & Policy.*
Available at: http://www.yale.edu/webmaster/elsinore.guidelines.html

Additional Chapter Notes:
To promote the statewide networking infrastructure initiative known as Access Indiana, the state of Indiana established in 1995 an Internet Grant Program to provide financial assistance for school corporations seeking a direct connection to the Internet (as opposed to dial-up access). Managed by Intelenet, a non-profit state commission, the program will disburse $10,000 matching grants to public schools in Indiana to pay for the following:

1. Recurring service fees, as well as installation fees, paid to an Internet Preferred Transport Provider (PTP)
2. One-time hardware/software acquisition or commercial services setup, specifically required to deliver the Internet service.
3. Faculty and Technology staff training required to ensure productive use of the Internet connection within the school corporation.

See Intelenet Commission Internet Grant Program for Indiana School Corporations.
Available at: http://ideanet.doe.state.in.us/htmls/guide.html and

Memo from Dr. Suellen Reed to Superintendents of Indiana Public School Corporations. (1 December 1995).
Available at: http://ideanet.doe.state.in.us/htmls/let.html

CHAPTER FOUR

Hert, C.A., H. Rosenbaum, S. M. Backs. 1995. *Information needs and uses during Internet training*. Proceedings of the American Society for Information Science, National Meetings. Vol. 58.

Jakob, D. 1995. Finding Information on the Web.
Available at: http://www.nlc-bnc.ca/pubs/netnotes/notes15.htm

Leonard, A. 1996. Where to find anything on the net. *c|net*.
Available at: http://www.cnet.com/Content/Reviews/Compare/Search/

Liu, J. 1996. Understanding WWW Search Tools.
Available at: http://www.indiana.edu/~librcsd/search/

Scoville, R. 1996. Find it on the Net. *PC World*. 14 (1), pp.125-130.
Available at: http://www.pcworld.com/reprints/lycos.htm

Webster, K. and K. Paul. 1996. Beyond Surfing: Tools and Techniques for Searching the Web. *Information Technology*.
Available at: http://magi.com/~mmelick/it96jan.htm

CHAPTER FIVE

Anderson, R.H., T. K. Bikson, S. A. Law, and B. M. Mitchell. 1996. *Universal access to e-mail: Feasibility and societal implications*. RAND Corporation.
Available at http://www.rand.org:80/publications/MR/MR650/mr650.ch1/ch1.html

Avis, A. 1995. *Public Spaces on the Information Highway: The Role of Community Networks*. Thesis Submitted To The Faculty Of Graduate Program In Communication Studies. University of Calgary, Calgary, Alberta
Available at http://www.ucalgary.ca/UofC/faculties/GNST/theses/avis/thesis.html

Berners-Lee, T. 1994. Request for Comments: 1630— Universal Resource Identifiers in WWW: A Unifying Syntax for the Expression of Names and Addresses of Objects on the Network as used in the World-Wide Web. Network Working Group
Available at ftp://ds.internic.net/rfc/rfc1630.txt

Bertot, J.C., C. R. McClure, and D. L. Zweizig. 1996. The 1996 National Survey of Public Libraries and the Internet: Progress and Issues: Final Report. National Commission on Libraries and Information Sciences.
Available at http://istweb.syr.edu/Project/Faculty/McClure-NSPL96/NSPL96_2.html

Cronin, M.J. 1994. *Doing Business on the Internet: How the Electronic Highway is Transforming American Companies*. New York, NY: Van Nostrand Reinhold, p. 8.

Decouchant, D., V. Quint, and M. R. Salcedo. 1995. Structured cooperative authoring on the World Wide Web.
Available at http://www.w3.org/pub/WWW/Journal/1/quint.091/paper/091.html

GVU's WWW Surveying Team. 1996. GVU's 5th WWW User Survey. Graphics, Visualization, & Usability Center, College of Computing. Georgia Institute of Technology.
Available at http://www.cc.gatech.edu/gvu/user_surveys/survey-04-1996/#exec

International Federation of Library Associations and Institutions. 1996. Digital Libraries Resources, Research and Projects. This site contains a listing of Web and print-based resources about digital libraries and the NSF/NASA sponsored Digital Libraries Initiative.
Available at http://www.nlc-bnc.ca/ifla/II/diglib.htm

Internet Public Library. 1996. Internet Public Library MOO Introduction.
Available at http://www.ipl.org/moo/

LeFurgy, B. 1996. Net sells books. *Culture in Cyberspace*. 1(28).
Available at http://www.radix.net/~wlefurgy/cinc28.htm

Meeker, M. and C. DePuy. 1996. *The Internet Report*. New York, NY: Harper Business, p. 2-3.

Miller, S.E. 1994. The Network Observer. 1(8).
Available at http://communication.ucsd.edu/pagre/tno/august-1994.html#building

Ragget, D. 1994. The future of HTML and the WWW.
Available at http://r703a.chem.nthu.edu.tw/~ks/docs/www/htmlplus/hpwww94.html

Ruby, D. 1996. The future of the net. c|net.com
Available at: http://www.cnet.com/Content/Features/Dlife/Future/ss02.html

United States Advisory Council on the National Information Infrastructure. 1996. *A Nation of Opportunity: A Final Report of the United States Advisory Council on the National Information Infrastructure.*
Available at http://www.benton.org/Library/KickStart/nation.impact.html

Additional Chapter Notes:

There are many sources you can use for Internet statistics, although the reliability of these estimates must always be taken with a grain of salt. Some useful sources include these:

FIND/SVP. 1996. The American Internet User Survey.
Available at http://etrg.findsvp.com/features/newinet.html

O'Reilly & Associates. 1995. Defining the Internet Opportunity.
Available at http://www.ora.com/research/users/charts/pop-proj.html

Ruby, D. 1996. The future of the net. c|net.com
Available at http://www.cnet.com/Content/Features/Dlife/Future/Stats/ss13.html

There are hundreds of projects that are integrating the Internet into all facets of education at all levels. A sampling of these projects include:

The Global Schoolhouse's Internet Project Registry, a site sponsored by Walden University, intended for busy teachers searching for appropriate on-line projects to integrate into their required coursework. The Registry is a site where teachers can find projects from the Global SchoolNet Foundation (GSN) and other organizations such as I*EARN, IECC, NASA, GLOBE, Academy One, TIES, Tenet, TERC, as well as countless outstanding projects conducted by classroom teachers all over the world.
Available at http://www.gsn.org/gsn/proj/index.html

The History/Social Studies Web Site for K-12 Teachers, which provides access to a range of resources in history and social studies, as well as information about use of the Internet for teaching and resource purposes.
Available at http://www.execpc.com/~dboals/boals.html

The Incredible Art Department, maintained by Ken Rohrer, an Indiana elementary and middle school art teacher, contains a lesson plan section with over 20 lesson plans, submitted by elementary, middle school, high school, and college art teachers. There are links to school art on the Net, a selected monthly

school art room, featuring a gallery of that school's work, elementary, secondary, and higher education art rooms and departments ("Art Stuff"), and a pointer to an art "site of the week."
Available at http://www.artswire.org/kenroar/

See the Web site maintained by the Morino Institute, which "is dedicated to opening the doors of opportunity— economic, civic, health, and education— and empowering people to improve their lives and communities in the Communications Age. The Institute helps individuals and institutions harness the power of information and the potential of interactive communications as tools for overcoming the challenges that face them." There is an extensive listing of useful resources concerned with community networking and the Internet.
Available at http://www.morino.org/

NASA's Online Educational Resources, a part of the mission of the High Performance Computing and Communications program, whose purpose it is to foster increased use of new computer and networking technologies to help support accelerated learning programs in education. These rough listings provide pointers to some online resources for students and educators, as well as to projects that address these goals.
Available at http://quest.arc.nasa.gov/OER/

The Science Information Infrastructure (SII) project, which is a collaboration among teachers and scientists. The SII is developing resources using NASA images and data covering topics such as ozone depletion, satellites, auroras, and more.
Available at http://www.exploratorium.edu/learning_studio/sii/

Two excellent sources of current information about domestic and international attempts to regulate the Internet are

The Electronic Frontier Foundation (EFF), which maintains a "Global, International & Non-US Issues & Policy Archive" containing a growing "collection of international net-censorship reports, from the fight-censorship mailing list . . . [with] . . . extensive background on global efforts to muzzle the Net."
Available at http://www.eff.org/pub/Global/

The Electronic Privacy Information Center (EPIC), which "is a public interest research center in Washington, D.C. It was established in 1994 to focus public attention on emerging civil liberties issues and to protect privacy, the First Amendment, and constitutional values."
Available at http://www.epic.org/

Two extensive sources for information about copyright, privacy, and the protection of intellectual property in the digital realm are

The EFF's "Intellectual Property Online: Patent, Trademark, Copyright Archive" which contains an extensive list of resources concerned with intellectual property issues.
Available at http://www.eff.org/pub/Intellectual_property/#files

A 1995 report by the IITF Working Group on Intellectual Property Rights. "Intellectual Property and the National Information Infrastructure: The Report of the Working Group on Intellectual Property Rights"
Available at http://www.uspto.gov/web/offices/com/doc/ipnii

Some examples of technical and practical work on problems deterring business growth on the Internet include:

CyberCash Home Page.
Available at http://www.cybercash.com

DigiCash Corporation Home Page.
Available at: http://www.digicash.com

First Virtual Home Page.
Available at http://www.fv.com

Peirce, M. and D. O'Mahony. 1995. Scalable, Secure Cash Payment for WWW: Resources with the PayMe Protocol Set
Available at http://www.w3.org/pub/WWW/Journal/1/omahony.228/paper/228.html

Credits

American Library Association's Office for Intellectual Freedom
Judith Krug, Director
http://www.ala.org

Bellingham School District 501, Bellingham, Washington
Jamieson McKenzie, Director of Libraries, Media and Technology
Policies reproduced with permission from the Bellingham Public Schools
http://www.bham.wednet.edu/

Chris Olson & Associates
A full-service marketing firm, specializing in promoting the services and products of libraries, information service professionals, and information-based companies.
Library icons by Chris Olson
http://www.chrisolson.com

Dailey, David, Informational Computing Officer, Williams College
"Simple Rule Generation Paradigm" graphic by David Dailey
http://www.williams.edu/Policies/

Entertainment CAD Services
Joseph Champelli, Director. Created "the *Neal-Schuman WebMaster*"
http://members.aol.com/entcadds/index.html
(joechamp@wizcred.com)

Florida International University
"World Wide Web Policies," Copyright 1996 Florida International University
http://www.fiu.edu/webpolicy.html

Hill, Charles, Assistant Superintendent Putnam Valley Schools, Putnam Valley, New York
For further information, contact Charles Hill (chill@putwest.boces.org)
http://putwest.boces.org

Ingram, Catherine. "A Public Librarian's Guide to Internet Access"
http://www.inil.com/users/caingram/cl_index.htm

Indiana Department of Education's Division of Educational Information Systems
Mike Huffman, Director
http://ideanet.doe.state.in.us/

Indiana University
"Computer Users' Privileges and Responsibilities," Copyright 1996, The Trustees of Indiana University
http://www.indiana.edu/~ucspubs/iu001/

International Federation of Library Associations' Bibliographic Standard Icon Set
Project Head Bruce Royan, Director of Information Services and University Librarian, University of Stirling, Scotland
http://lorne.stir.ac.uk/iconstd/

Lawrence Public Library, Lawrence, Kansas
Bruce Flanders, Director
http://www.idir.net/~lpl/

Leita, Carole— Berkeley Public Library, Berkeley California
http://www.ci.berkeley.ca.us/bpl

InfoPeople Project, California State Library
http://www.lib.berkeley.edu:8000/index.html

Levine, Jennifer—"Jenny's Cybrary to the Stars"
http://sashimi.wwa.com/~jayhawk/index.html

Minnesota Coalition Against Censorship
Fran McDonald, Ph.D. (President)

Monroe County Community School Corporation, Bloomington, Indiana 47401

David A. Frye, Ph.D., Associate Superintendent for Instruction
Carl Zager, Instructional Technology Coordinator
http://www.mccsc.edu

Morton Grove Public Library, Morton Grove, Illinois
Kevin Justie, Head of Technical and Automated Services
"WEBrary is a trademark of the Morton Grove Public Library"
http://www.nslsilus.org/mgkhome/

Public Web Project
Dr. Thom Gillespie, Professor of Library and Information Science, Indiana University, Bloomington, with:
Karla Alexander, Candice Bertotti, Dung-lan Chen, Sheau-hui Ching, Norico Hara, Huey-ying Hsu, Christopher Jackson, Rosemary Lovely, Tim Jones and Brett Pfingston.
http://www.indiana.edu/~slizzard/pwp/pwp.html

Ralph, Randy D., MLIS, Ph.D.
Technical Consultant and Trainer
http://www.netstrider.com/randy/

Saint Joseph County Public Library, South Bend, Indiana
Donald Napoli, Director
http://sjcpl.lib.in.us

Schrock, Kathleen—"Kathy Schrock's Guide for Educators"
Web site created 6/95 by Kathleen Schrock
(kschrock@capecod.net)
http://www.capecod.net/Schrockguide/

Sears, Bill—California State Telementor and Library/Information Technology Teacher for Mesa Verde High School, California
http://www.sanjuan.edu/schools.mesaverde/libtech/libtech.htm

Stull, Nina and Mapes, Bruce of Newark Memorial High School, Newark, California
Library Home Page constructed by Nina Stull, Librarian and Bruce Mapes, Technician.
http://www.infolane.com/nm-library

University of Houston Libraries
Nancy Buchanan, Coordinator of Electronic Resources
Copyright University of Houston Libraries
http://info.lib.uh.edu/

Werbach, Kevin—"The Bare Bones Guide to HTML"
Copyright1995, 1996 Kevin Werbach
http://werbach.com

Appendix A

Text of the Communications Decency Act

The document provided in this appendix, the Telecommunications Act of 1996, which was passed by the U.S. Congress on February 1, 1996 is available at the following site:

http://www.technologylaw.com/techlaw/telecom_bill.html

*Note: The U.S. Supreme Court is expected to rule on the constitutionality of this Act in July, 1997.

SEC. 230. PROTECTION FOR PRIVATE BLOCKING AND SCREENING OF OFFENSIVE MATERIAL.

(a) Findings: The Congress finds the following—

(1) The rapidly developing array of Internet and other interactive computer services available to individual Americans represents an extraordinary advance in the availability of educational and informational resources to our citizens.

(2) These services offer users a great degree of control over the information that they receive, as well as the potential for even greater control in the future as technology develops.

(3) The Internet and other interactive computer services offer a forum for a true diversity of political discourse, unique opportunities for cultural development, and myriad avenues for intellectual activity.

(4) The Internet and other interactive computer services have flourished, to the benefit of all Americans, with a minimum of government regulation.

Increasingly Americans are relying on interactive media or a variety of political, educational, cultural, and entertainment services.

(b) Policy: It is the policy of the United States—
  (1) to promote the continued development of the Internet and other interactive computer services and other interactive media;
  (2) to preserve the vibrant and competitive free market that presently exists for the Internet and other interactive computer services, unfettered by Federal or State regulation;
  (3) to encourage the development of technologies which maximize user control over what information is received by individuals, families, and schools who use the Internet and other interactive computer services;
  (4) to remove disincentives for the development and utilization of blocking and filtering technologies that empower parents to restrict their children's access to objectionable or inappropriate online material; and
  (5) to ensure vigorous enforcement of Federal criminal laws to deter and punish trafficking in obscenity, stalking, and harassment by means of computer.

SEC. 502. OBSCENE OR HARASSING USE OF TELCOMMUNICATIONS FACILITIES.

Whoever—
(1) in interstate or foreign communications knowingly
  (A) uses an interactive computer service to send to a specific person or persons under 18 years of age, or
  (B) uses any interactive computer service to display in a manner available to a person under 18 years of age, any comment, request, suggestion, proposal, image, or other communication that, in context, depicts or describes, in terms patently offensive as measured by contemporary community standards, sexual or excretory activities or organs, regardless of whether the user of such service placed the call or initiated the communication; or
(2) knowingly permits any telecommunications facility under such person's control to be used for an activity prohibited by paragraph (1) with the intent that it be used for such activity, shall be fined under title 18, United States Code, or imprisoned not more than two years, or both.

TITLE V—OBSCENITY AND VIOLENCE

Subtitle A—Obscene, Harassing, and Wrongful Utilization of Telecommunications Facilities

SEC. 501. SHORT TITLE: This title may be cited as the "Communications Decency Act of 1996".

SEC. 502. OBSCENE OR HARASSING USE OF TELECOMMUNICATIONS FACILITIES UNDER THE COMMUNICATIONS ACT OF 1934.

Section 223 (47 U.S.C. 223) is amended—

(1) by striking subsection (a) and inserting in lieu thereof:

(a) Whoever—

(1) in interstate or foreign communications—

(A) by means of a telecommunications device knowingly—

(i) makes, creates, or solicits, and

(ii) initiates the transmission of, any comment, request, suggestion, proposal, image, or other communication which is obscene, lewd, lascivious, filthy, or indecent, with intent to annoy, abuse, threaten, or harass another person;

(B) by means of a telecommunications device knowingly—

(i) makes, creates, or solicits, and

(ii) initiates the transmission of, any comment, request, suggestion, proposal, image, or other communication which is obscene or indecent, knowing that the recipient of the communication is under 18 years of age, regardless of whether the maker of such communication placed the call or initiated the communication;

(C) makes a telephone call or utilizes a telecommunications device, whether or not conversation or communication ensues, without disclosing his identity and with intent to annoy, abuse, threaten, or harass any person at the called number or who receives the communications;

(D) makes or causes the telephone of another repeatedly or continuously to ring, with intent to harass any person at the called number; or

(E) makes repeated telephone calls or repeatedly initiates communication with a telecommunications device, during which conversation or communication ensues, solely to harass any person at the called number or who receives the communication; or

(2) knowingly permits any telecommunications facility under his control to be used for any activity prohibited by paragraph

(1) with the intent that it be used for such activity, shall be fined under title 18, United States Code, or imprisoned not more than two years, or both; and

(2) by adding at the end the following new subsections:

(d) Whoever—

(1) in interstate or foreign communications knowingly—

(A) uses an interactive computer service to send to a specific person or persons under 18 years of age, or

(B) uses any interactive computer service to display in a manner available to a person under 18 years of age, any comment, request, suggestion, proposal, image, or other communication that, in context, depicts or describes, in terms patently offensive as measured by contemporary community standards, sexual or excretory activities or organs, regardless of whether the user of such service placed the call or initiated the communication; or

(2) knowingly permits any telecommunications facility under such person's control to be used for an activity prohibited by paragraph (1) with the intent that it be used for such activity, shall be fined under title 18, United States Code, or imprisoned not more than two years, or both.

(e) In addition to any other defenses available by law:

(1) No person shall be held to have violated subsection (a) or (d) solely for providing access or connection to or from a facility, system, or network not under that person's control, including transmission, downloading, intermediate storage, access software, or other related capabilities that are incidental to providing such access or connection that does not include the creation of the content of the communication.

(2) The defenses provided by paragraph (1) of this subsection shall not be applicable to a person who is a conspirator with an entity actively involved in the creation or knowing distribution of communications that violate this section, or who knowingly advertises the availability of such communications.

(3) The defenses provided in paragraph (1) of this subsection shall not be applicable to a person who provides access or connection to a facility, system, or network engaged in the violation of this section that is owned or controlled by such person.

(4) No employer shall be held liable under this section for the actions of an employee or agent unless the employee's or agent's conduct is within the scope of his or her employment or agency and the employer (A) having knowledge of such conduct, authorizes or ratifies such conduct, or (B) recklessly disregards such conduct.

(5) It is a defense to a prosecution under subsection (a)(1)(B) or (d), or under subsection (a)(2) with respect to the use of a facility for an activity under subsection (a)(1)(B) that a person—

(A) has taken, in good faith, reasonable, effective, and appropriate actions under the circumstances to restrict or prevent access by minors to a communication specified in such subsections, which may involve any appropriate measures to restrict minors from such communications, including any method which is feasible under available technology; or

(B) has restricted access to such communication by requiring use of a verified credit card, debit account, adult access code, or adult personal identification number.

(6) The Commission may describe measures which are reasonable, effective, and appropriate to restrict access to prohibited communications under subsection (d). Nothing in this section authorizes the Commission to enforce, or is intended to provide the Commission with the authority to approve, sanction, or permit, the use of such measures. The Commission shall have no enforcement authority over the failure to utilize such measures. The Commission shall not endorse specific products relating to such measures. The use of such measures shall be admitted as evidence of good faith efforts for purposes of paragraph (5) in any action arising under subsection (d). Nothing in this section shall be construed to treat interactive computer services as common carriers or telecommunications carriers.

(f) (1) No cause of action may be brought in any court or administrative agency against any person on account of any activity that is not in violation of any law punishable by criminal or civil penalty, and that the person has taken in good faith to implement a defense authorized under this section or otherwise to restrict or prevent the transmission of, or access to, a communication specified in this section.

(2) No State or local government may impose any liability for commercial activities or actions by commercial entities, nonprofit libraries, or institutions of higher education in connection with an activity or action described in subsection (a)(2) or (d) that is inconsistent with the treatment of those activities or actions under this section: Provided, however, That nothing herein shall preclude any State or local government from enacting and enforcing complementary oversight, liability, and regulatory systems, procedures, and requirements, so long as such systems, procedures, and requirements govern only intrastate services and do not result in the imposition of inconsistent rights, duties or obligations on the provision of interstate services. Nothing in this subsection shall preclude any State or local government from governing conduct not covered by this section.

(g) Nothing in subsection (a), (d), (e), or (f) or in the defenses to prosecution under (a) or (d) shall be construed to affect or limit the application or enforcement of any other Federal law.

(h) For purposes of this section—
  (1) The use of the term 'telecommunications device' in this section—
    (A) shall not impose new obligations on broadcasting station licensees and cable operators covered by obscenity and indecency provisions elsewhere in this Act; and
    (B) does not include an interactive computer service.
  (2) The term 'interactive computer service' has the meaning provided in section 230(e)(2).
  (3) The term 'access software' means software (including client or server software) or enabling tools that do not create or provide the content of the communication but that allow a user to do any one or more of the following:
    (A) filter, screen, allow, or disallow content; (B) pick, choose, analyze, or digest content; or (C) transmit, receive, display, forward, cache, search, subset, organize, reorganize, or translate content.
  (4) The term 'institution of higher education' has the meaning provided in section 1201 of the Higher Education Act of 1965 (20 U.S.C. 1141).
  (5) The term 'library' means a library eligible for participation in State-based plans for funds under title III of the Library Services and Construction Act (20 U.S.C. 355e et seq.).'

SEC. 507. CLARIFICATION OF CURRENT LAWS REGARDING COMMUNICATION OF OBSCENE MATERIALS THROUGH THE USE OF COMPUTERS.

(a) Importation or Transportation—Section 1462 of title 18, United States Code, is amended—
  (1) in the first undesignated paragraph, by inserting "or interactive computer service (as defined in section 230(e)(2) of the Communications Act of 1934)" after "carrier"; and
  (2) in the second undesignated paragraph—
    (A) by inserting "or receives," after "takes";
    (B) by inserting "or interactive computer service (as defined in section 230(e)(2) of the Communications Act of 1934)" after "common carrier"; and
    (C) by inserting "or importation" after "carriage". (b) Transportation for Purposes of Sale or Distribution. The first undesignated paragraph of section 1465 of title 18, United States Code, is amended—
      (1) by striking "transports in" and inserting "transports or travels in, or uses a facility or means of";
      (2) by inserting "or an interactive computer service (as defined in section 230(e)(2) of the Communications Act of 1934) in or affecting such com-

merce" after "foreign commerce" the first place it appears;

(3) by striking ", or knowingly travels in" and all that follows through "obscene material in interstate or foreign commerce," and inserting "of". (c) Interpretation.—The amendments made by this section are clarifying and shall not be interpreted to limit or repeal any prohibition contained in sections 1462 and 1465 of title 18, United States Code, before such amendment, under the rule established in United States v. Alpers, 338 U.S. 680 (1950).

SEC. 509. ONLINE FAMILY EMPOWERMENT.

Title II of the Communications Act of 1934 (47 U.S.C. 201 et seq.) is amended by adding at the end the following new section:

SEC. 230. PROTECTION FOR PRIVATE BLOCKING AND SCREENING OF OFFENSIVE MATERIAL.

(a) Findings.—The Congress finds the following:
  (1) The rapidly developing array of Internet and other interactive computer services available to individual Americans represent an extraordinary advance in the availability of educational and informational resources to our citizens.
  (2) These services offer users a great degree of control over the information that they receive, as well as the potential for even greater control in the future as technology develops.
  (3) The Internet and other interactive computer services offer a forum for a true diversity of political discourse, unique opportunities for cultural development, and myriad avenues for intellectual activity.
  (4) The Internet and other interactive computer services have flourished, to the benefit of all Americans, with a minimum of government regulation.
  (5) Increasingly Americans are relying on interactive media for a variety of political, educational, cultural, and entertainment services.

(b) Policy.—It is the policy of the United States—
  (1) to promote the continued development of the Internet and other interactive computer services and other interactive media;
  (2) to preserve the vibrant and competitive free market that presently exists for the Internet and other interactive computer services, unfettered by Federal or State regulation;
  (3) to encourage the development of technologies which maximize user control over what information is received by individuals, families, and schools who use the Internet and other interactive computer services;
  (4) to remove disincentives for the development and utilization of blocking and filtering

technologies that empower parents to restrict their children's access to objectionable or inappropriate online material; and

(5) to ensure vigorous enforcement of Federal criminal laws to deter and punish trafficking in obscenity, stalking, and harassment by means of computer.

(c) Protection for 'Good Samaritan' Blocking and Screening of Offensive Material.—

(1) Treatment of publisher or speaker.—No provider or user of an interactive computer service shall be treated as the publisher or speaker of any information provided by another information content provider.

(2) Civil liability.—No provider or user of an interactive computer service shall be held liable on account of—

(A) any action voluntarily taken in good faith to restrict access to or availability of material that the provider or user considers to be obscene, lewd, lascivious, filthy, excessively violent, harassing, or otherwise objectionable, whether or not such material is constitutionally protected; or

(B) any action taken to enable or make available to information content providers or others the technical means to restrict access to material described in paragraph (1).

(d) Effect on Other Laws.—

(1) No effect on criminal law.—Nothing in this section shall be construed to impair the enforcement of section 223 of this Act, chapter 71 (relating to obscenity) or 110 (relating to sexual exploitation of children) of title 18, United States Code, or any other Federal criminal statute.

(2) No effect on intellectual property law.—Nothing in this section shall be construed to limit or expand any law pertaining to intellectual property.

(3) State law.—Nothing in this section shall be construed to prevent any State from enforcing any State law that is consistent with this section. No cause of action may be brought and no liability may be imposed under any State or local law that is inconsistent with this section.

(4) No effect on communications privacy law.—Nothing in this section shall be construed to limit the application of the Electronic Communications Privacy Act of 1986 or any of the amendments made by such Act, or any similar State law.

(e) Definitions.—As used in this section:

(1) Internet.—The term 'Internet' means the international computer network of both Federal and non-Federal interoperable packet switched data networks.

(2) Interactive computer service.—The term 'interactive computer service' means any information service, system, or access software provider that provides or enables computer access by multiple users to a computer server, including specifically a service or system that provides access to the Internet and such systems operated or services offered by libraries or educational institutions.

(3) Information content provider.—The term 'information content provider' means any person or entity that is responsible, in whole or in part, for the creation or develop-

ment of information provided through the Internet or any other interactive computer service.

(4) Access software provider.—The term 'access software provider' means a provider of software (including client or server software), or enabling tools that do any one or more of the following:

   (A) filter, screen, allow, or disallow content;
   (B) pick, choose, analyze, or digest content; or
   (C) transmit, receive, display, forward, cache, search, subset, organize, reorganize, or translate content.

Appendix B

References to Useful Materials

This appendix lists many different resources you may find useful as you work with your library's Web site. Please note that some of the annotations included here were taken directly from the Web pages of the references being discussed.

MANAGING WEB SITES

Liu, C., J. Peek, J. R. Jones, B. Buus, and A. Nye. 1994. *Managing Internet Information Services*. Sebastopol, CA: O'Reilly and Associates.

Stein, L. 1995. *How to Set Up and Maintain a World Wide Web Site: The Guide for Information Providers*. Reading, MA: Addison-Wesley.

Sullivan, D. 1997. A Webmaster's Guide to Search Engines. http://calafia.com/webmasters/
"Search engines are one of the primary ways that Internet users find Web sites. Every day, search engines 'crawl' the Web: they visit Web sites, then store the text of Web pages they find into giant catalogs. This allows Web users to enter a few keywords, push 'submit' and see what Web pages match their queries.

For Webmasters, understanding how search engines operate is necessary to ensure their sites are properly indexed. Good 'search engine design' is vital. Without it, a site may appear poorly in search engine rankings or not be indexed at all.

This site contains design tips and information about search engines that will help Webmasters optimize their sites for indexing. It is based on studies I have done, search engine help pages, articles, reviews, books, tips from others and additional information received directly from the various search engines."

SEARCH TOOLS

Gaer, S. 1996. Searching the World Wide Web.
http://www.otan.dni.us/webfarm/emailproject/search.htm
This is a Web version of a workshop prepared for the Research Department at Rancho Santiago College. It contains a useful description of searching techniques for a range of search engines and an excellent set of references for further exploration.

Koch, T. 1997. Browsing and Searching Internet Resources
http://www.ub2.lu.se/nav_menu.html

Northern Webs. 1996. The Search Engine Tutorial for Web Designers
http://www.digital-cafe.com/~webmaster/set01.html
"The Search Engine Tutorial for Web Designers explains how to design your pages, keeping the search engines in mind, and why it is necessary to do so. Knowledge is a powerful weapon and having knowledge of WHAT a search engine is going to do with your page, while you are designing it, allows you to build a better resulting Web page. A low graphics version of this site can be found here. Northern Webs is extremely pleased to acknowledge the award of NetGuide Gold Status to our Search Engine Tutorial. THANKS NETGUIDE!"

Tyner, R. 1997. Sink or Swim: Internet Search Tools & Techniques (Version 2.0)
http://oksw01.okanagan.bc.ca/libr/connect96/search.htm
"Imagine you are searching for information in the world's largest library, where the books and journals (stripped of their covers and title pages) are shelved in no particular order, and without reference to a central catalogue. A researcher's nightmare? Without question. The World Wide Web defined? Not exactly. Instead of a central catalogue, the Web offers the choice of dozens of different search tools, each with its own database, command language, search capabilities, and method of displaying results.

Given the above, the need is clear to familiarize oneself with a variety of search tools and to develop effective search techniques, if one hopes to take advantage of the resources offered by the Web without spending many fruitless hours flailing about, and eventually drowning, in a sea of irrelevant information."

TRAINING MATERIALS

Berkeley Public Library. 1996. Getting Started on the Internet
http://www.ci.berkeley.ca.us/bpl/files/gettings.html
"Welcome to our online guide to help you get started using the Public Internet access computers at the Berkeley Public Library!"

Burlington County Library. 1996. Netscape Tutorial at the Burlington County Library.
http://www.burlco.lib.nj.us/tutorial/
"Welcome! You are about to embark upon a strange and wonderful journey on the Internet, but first you need to learn how to use some tools to make effective use of your time. The program you're using now, called Netscape, is one of those tools. If you already know how to use Netscape, you can skip ahead to learn about the Internet itself. Otherwise, continue reading."

Cochran Interactive. 1997. Life on the Internet: Exploring
http://www.screen.com/understand/exploring.html
"The 'starting out' section of Exploring the Internet offers a basic overview of the Internet, a guide to subject indexes and search tools, and links to resources on "netiquette." In addition to covering the most commonly used Internet technologies, the "applications" section covers creating homepages, finding Internet software, and getting connected. Each page of resources is large, but the annotations will help the beginner find needed information quickly. Users may also participate in a forum on the Internet."

Computing and Network Services—Tutorials Page Learning Online!
http://www.ualberta.ca/~maldridg/tutor/Tutorials.html
This page just underwent a complete overhaul and has several dozen new links to Tutorials on the Web, with a lot more on the way. Subjects range from software such as Eudora and Netscape to Photo-Electronic Imaging.

December, J. 1997. Web Development Quality
http://www.december.com/web/develop/quality.html
Purpose: This Web site describes and collects references to resources about methodologies, techniques, and resources for developing high-quality World Wide Web-based information.

Contents: This site includes a description of a methodology for developing Web information as well as links to online resources to support this methodology's processes and elements.
A newly established sub-section of the Information Quality WWW Virtual Library, it is maintained by John December <decemj@rpi.edu>

Library of Congress. 1996. Internet Guides, Tutorials, and Training Information
http://lcweb.loc.gov/global/internet/training.html
An extensive collection of links to collections of Guides and Courses, Individual Guides and Courses, Internet Glossaries, and Resources for Internet Trainers

Morris City Library. 1996. MORENET
http://www.gti.net/mocolib1/morenet.html
"In August 1993 Bellcore and the Morris Automated Information Network (MAIN) launched a two year investigation of public access to the Internet. The project was the brainchild of Stephen and Judy Weinstein, he then at Bellcore, she a librarian at the Parsippany-Troy Hills (NJ) Public Library. Basic Internet services were provided to the entire county population of 430,000 on nearly 300 terminals in 32 public libraries. Some 200 library staff members and, on a first-come, first-serve basis, 174 library patrons, were given full Internet accounts, including e-mail, bulletin boards, newsgroups and an open telnet prompt, features missing from the online public access catalog (OPAC) feed. The system was, and remains, a text based system; Lynx is the Web browser. Because the Morris Educational and Research Network (MORENET) was, initially, an experiment, it was begun with no specific or special Internet access policies being written. By August 1995, when Bellcore's share in the project was over, the libraries of Morris County and the people they serve were so accustomed to the Internet as an information resource that MAIN opted to continue the access within the system online public catalog."

Newark Memorial High School Library. 1996. Tutorial for Internet Driver's License.
http://www.infolane.com/nm-library/itblcon.html
"This guide will help you get started using the Internet. Although you won't really be online, you will have the 'look and feel' of being online while you learn the skills to drive the information superhighway. You must successfully complete all the steps and pass the Internet Driving Test to earn the privilege of accessing the Internet at Newark Memorial High School Library. At the end of

this tutorial is an Internet Driver's License which you and your parents/guardians must sign and return to the librarian."

Nordic Centre of Excellence for Electronic Publishing. 1996. Cookbook for Creating WWW Publications
http://www.vtt.fi/inf/nordep/projects/webpilot/cookbook/
"First of all, learn HTML (HyperText Markup Language). It's not too difficult, and there is nothing mystic in it. In HTML, you just insert tags (element names delimited from the content of the document with < and >) into your documents. A tag defines where an element starts, where it ends and what is the role of that part of the document, instead of defining how it should look. (Produced by Nordic Centre of Excellence for Electronic Publishing, VTT Information Service, Finland)"

Santa Cruz Public Library. 1996. Where do I begin?
http://www.cruzio.com/~sclibs/where/where.html
"The Basics—Tutorials: If you are a novice and don't know how to move around on the World Wide Web, it is a good idea to start with one of the basic tutorials: Basic Netscape Tutorial; Basic Lynx Tutorial

Starting Places on the World Wide Web: If you already know how to move around and want to get started, we can suggest some ways to begin, depending upon what you want to do. If you want to: Look for a Specific Subject; Get an Idea What There Is on the Internet."

UNIX SKILLS

Taylor, D. 1995. *Teach Yourself UNIX in a Week*. Indianapolis, IN: SAMS Publishing.

University of Washington. 1996. Welcome to the University of Washington's Pine Information Center.
http://www.cac.washington.edu/pine/
Pine®—a Program for Internet News & Email— is a tool for reading, sending, and managing electronic messages. Pine was designed by the Office of Computing & Communications at the University of Washington specifically with novice computer users in mind, but it can be tailored to accommodate the needs of "power users" as well.

Appendix C

New Users' FAQ

Expect updates to this document by Rick Gates. Check on the Internet for them.

Commonly Asked Questions When Conducting Internet Training
Rick Gates— Net Assets (rgates@locust.cic.net)
November 1, 1995
http://www.sir.arizona.edu/rick/conduct.html

QUESTIONS

What is the Internet?

It doesn't get more basic than this . . . You can talk about how the Internet is a large, distributed collection of computers from a variety of manufacturers, all running TCP/IP.

But that seems to leave a lot of blank looks.

Or you can tell them that the Internet is a hierarchy of networks, that is, a network of networks of networks of networks of . . .

. . . and that's where I usually begin. I've found that a good way to help novices understand what the Internet is, is to draw a simple path that a mail message follows as it moves from a user in a university to a user in a big business. The mail message necessarily moves throughout the hierarchy of networks, thereby illuminating the underlying structure. Since I begin with a university, I also set the stage for showing the history of how the Internet was built.

That's the infrastructure . . . I also try to teach users that the Internet is a society. I do this by posing a question, "How do we learn about societies?" The answer is that we learn about societies by living in them, not by reading about them in a book. It's the same with the Internet.

Who's in charge?

I like to tell novices that they're in charge. To a large extent, this is true. But then I explain that the Internet was built from the bottom up, with every network agreeing to carry its share of the load.

But then I tell them that the Internet couldn't exist without some agreement on how it all works. That's when I tell them about groups like the Internet Engineering Task Force, with its focus on good code, built from the ground up, and the InterNIC, insuring the unique addresses of the Domain Name System.

How can I do this from home?

I explain that the Internet is such a hot topic that everybody is interested in getting connected. As a result, the once small industry of local Internet service providers is growing at an astronomic rate. Unless you live in a very small town, it's highly likely that you'll be able to make a local phone call to a provider which will connect you to the Internet.

How do I find the time to learn all this?

This is one of the toughest questions to answer. In one way, you don't find the time, you make the time. We all have priorities in our jobs. We have priorities at home. The best suggestion that I can make here is to dedicate some small percentage of time to a trial period, where you can see if the Internet would be valuable to your work or home life. Then, if you make the decision that it's really not worth it, you can set it aside. Later, if the Nets grow to the point where it becomes more important, you'll already have some experience.

How do I convince my boss that the Internet is worth my time?

A great way to convince superiors in a business that this is all worth taking a look at, is to use the great analogy in Douglas Comer's *The Internet Book*.

Douglas loads us on a time machine and transports us back in this country 100 years. Knowing everything that we do about 1995, our job is to go to a businessman of 1895 and try to sell him telephone service.

We'd tell him about how it would allow him to better communicate with suppliers and customers. But he'd tell us that the phone system in his county is pretty buggy, slow, and doesn't always work with the system in the county where his supplier is . . . and that very few of his customers have telephones.

In essence, it comes down to this . . . if very few have telephones, a telephone system is nothing more than an idle curiosity for the rich. If everybody has telephones, the system becomes a crucial tool.

Where are we today in the Internet? We're small in terms of universal service, but the growth rates are very high. Where will we be tomorrow? Ask your boss that.

Another good way to get your boss on board is to find out what her hobbies/interests are. Information coverage on the Net is very broad (not deep), and there's a very good chance that you'll be able to find your boss something personally interesting, and perhaps others that share similar interests. Often times, this hook is enough.

Where do I get tech support and training?

The answer to this question depends on the kind of access they have. If users are getting access through their organization, then it's usually the duty of somebody within that organization to provide support. However, dealing with these people can sometimes be a nightmare, in part because they're usually even busier than you are, and they're often isolated and unaware of what the users' perspectives are.

My suggestion is that you always approach local support personnel with two tasks done completely . . . First, if you are experiencing problems, write down all possible information about the problem, when it occurred, what you were doing, what software you were running, and very important . . . what error messages you encountered. These might not make sense to you, but they're crucial when trying to diagnose difficulties.

Secondly, document and show your support personnel that you've tried at least something to resolve the problem on your own . . . you'll get a lot better support from them if you show a willingness to try to solve things, thereby saving them some time.

If you're connecting from home with a local service provider I would urge you to be tough on them. Require excellent tech support. They're in a very fast growing and competitive industry, and they understand that the level of tech support they provide may make a bigger difference to their success than competitive pricing. Demand only the best.

Where do we find the money to access it?

These are fiscally tough times, and this is another tough question. Again, I would urge you to look at the charge of your organization, particularly the information and communications components. If these would be aided by accessing the Internet, you're half-way there.

As to digging up pots of money, we're in luck in one sense . . . the Internet is still a very new place and a very hot topic. Grants and other gifts are generally easier to get for technologies that are new than for established technologies.

How much does access cost?

Again this depends on your method of connection. Generally speaking, the greater the bandwidth you purchase, the greater your costs. Thus dial-up connections are the cheapest, and run anywhere from $10 to $30 per month.

Connecting more than an individual usually means higher bandwidth dedicated lines/service. This can run an organization anywhere from $100 to $3000 a month depending on the type of service and how many people you're trying to connect. Contact service providers for more details.

How much does support cost?

Once again, dial-up access for an individual generally comes with support built in from your service provider.

Connecting many users generally means connecting an existing network to the Internet. Thus your local network gurus usually (for better or worse), end up becoming your Internet support personnel. Your costs are a function of how well you support them.

What is TCP/IP?

I like to start this off by explaining that there are a lot of different types of computers connected to the Internet. For historical and proprietary reasons, few of these computers can automatically communicate with each other. Just because you've put a wire between an IBM mainframe and a Macintosh, it doesn't mean the two machines will talk to each other.

Because each computer is different, we need an agreed upon set of rules that allow computers to talk to each other. We'd need lots of these rules because we'd need to tell each computer how many bytes of data to send at a time, how to resend missing data, what the address of another computer looks like, who has access to what data, and hundreds of other details.

The rules for handling the details of computer-to-computer communication over the Internet is known as TCP/IP.

The big thing for novices to remember is that if a computer is to be a part of the Internet, it needs to be running the TCP/IP software in order to be able to communicate with all the other computers.

How do I get Internet software if I don't have Internet software?

Tough one. If you get access from a local service provider, it's their job to supply you with the initial set of shareware/freeware that you'll need to get started. If you're in an organizational setting go to the local network guru (remember to genuflect).

How do we guard against viruses?

The same way we always have . . . through the use of freeware/shareware/commercial products that we can use to test all software that we download before use. Practice safe sex, 'er computing.

Do people really do this for free?

Yes they do. People are liable to spend a lot of time educating others about any issue they feel passionately about. It's no different in the Internet; it's just reusable. Some people provide content on the Internet because they feel that they'll get other things in return, such as academic acclaim, notoriety, or millions in speaking fees (grin).

What are the rules for using the Net?

The rules of good behavior on the Nets are much like the rules in the society around us . . . few are legislated, many are articulated. We know them when we see them broken.

How do I find an e-mail address for user X?

This is one of the most difficult things to do on the Net. Because the Internet is distributed, it's difficult to find people. Your local phone company is in charge of local phone access so they can provide the white pages. There is no such company in charge of the Internet.

How do I find organization X on the Net?

This is a bit easier to do because each organization that wishes to maintain a Net presence needs to register their unique address with the InterNIC. This keeps all names in the Domain Name System unique. When they register, they need to provide contact and location information. This can be searched with tools such as Whois.

Also, a good rule of thumb is to put the string 'www' in front of a like domain. Thus putting 'www' in front of 'arizona.edu' gets you to the University of Arizona home page, and putting 'www' in front of 'ibm.com' gets you to the IBM home page.

Is it true that my kids can get pornography?

Yes, it's true . . . but it's not the kind of thing that will jump out at them . . . they'll need to go looking for it.

There are a couple of options available here . . . the first, and most important, is education. Teaching children that the society of the Internet has some of the same pitfalls and dark corners as the society around us is a valuable lesson.

Secondly, there has been a lot of growth over the last few months in the development of "filtering" software that allows parents to prevent access to certain sites. I recommend only the purchase of software that allows parents to educate themselves and selectively choose what their children have access to.

How do I find a service provider?

Connect to http://thelist.com/

OK, so I'm in Germany now, right?

A common misconception in the Internet is that the user is "resident," or located in a particular geographic location, jumping around the world.

I like to explain what client server is, telling them that they never really "go" anywhere, but are sending out requests for documents to places around the world.

What's a FAQ?

The Frequently Asked Questions (FAQ) files from the Usenet are one of the most underutilized resources on the Net. I like to tell novices how these are built by experts to protect themselves from "newbie" questions, and that they end up providing quite good encyclopedic information.

I usually access them at: ftp://rtfm.mit.edu/pub/usenet-by-hierarchy/

Appendix D

Frameset Translation

<HTML>	Here's the opening HTML tag.
<HEAD>	This opens the header.
<TITLE>Frames Demo</TITLE>	This is the title.
</HEAD>	This closes the header.
<FRAMESET COLS= "40%,60%">	This splits window into two unequal columns.
<FRAMESET ROWS= "30%,70%">	This splits first column into two unequal rows.
<FRAME SRC="frame1.htm">	This names the top cell in the first column.
<FRAME SRC="frame2.htm">	This names the bottom cell in the first column.
</FRAMESET>	This closes the frameset that defines the rows.
<FRAMESET ROWS= "25%,25%,25%,25%">	This splits second column into four equal rows.

<FRAME SRC="frame3.htm">	This names the top cell in the second column.
<FRAME SRC="frame4.htm">	This names the second cell in the second column.
<FRAME SRC="frame5.htm">	This names the third cell in the second column.
<FRAME SRC="frame6.htm">	This names the bottom cell in the second column.
</FRAMESET>	This closes the frameset that defines the rows.
</FRAMESET>	This closes frameset defining entire frame display.
</HTML>	This is the closing HTML tag.

Index

Acceptable Use Policies (AUP) xii, xiii, xiv, xxi, 2, 47–79
  Security issues 52–53
  Template 77–79
ACLU 33–34
Aesop's Fables 54
Aldritch, M. 91
Alldred, J. 100
American Library Association (ALA) xix, 39, 40, 42, 43, 47, 49, 50, 51, 53, 57, 62, 64, 66, 75, 76, 77, 79, 147
American Society for Information Science (ASIS) 87
Andressen, Marc xvii
Apple Computer 49
ARCHIE 90, 93, 94
Argus Associates 24
ASCII 11
Association of Research Libraries (ARL) 121
AT&T 122
Avis, A. 112

Beck, Terry 28
Bellingham Public Schools 18, 58, 59, 147
Berkeley Public Library 27, 66, 69, 148
Berners-Lee, Tim xi, 116
Bertland, Linda 6
Bertot, John Carlo xxi, 108
Bible 35
Birren, Faber 21
Boulder Public Library 4
BrowserWatch 121
Broyles, Linda 69
Bryant, Eugenia 28
Buchanon, Nancy 56, 149
Burger, Robert 51

California InFoPeople Project 52
Canby Public Library 73–74
Castro, E. 98, 99
CAUSE 121
Cavazos, E.A. 40
CD-ROM supplement (enclosed) xi, xiii, xiv, xv, xvi, xxii, 1, 6, 8, 10, 11, 14, 15, 21, 22, 27, 29, 38, 50, 52, 56, 65, 74, 75, 76, 77, 84, 88, 89
Censorship 31, 34, 36, 57–58, 70–75, 113
Center for Civic Networking xix
CGI (Common Gateway Interface) 9, 10, 45, 84
Champelli, Lisa 46
Cisler, Steve 49, 51
Civille, Richard xix
Clarence H. Rosa Public Library 50
Clinton, President William 32, 33, 46
Coalition for Networked Information 121
Color: A Survey in Words and Pictures 21

Communications Decency Act (Telecommunications Act of 1996) 33–35, 54, 107, 113, 151–159
Computer Professionals for Social Responsibility 111
Connecting to the Internet xi
Cookies 114
Cool Tool of the Day 121
Copyright xiii, xiv, 22, 31, 45, 79
Cronin, M.J. 114
CyberDewey 28
CyberPatrol 70–71

December, John 2, 99
Decouchant, D. 117
DePuy, C. 109
Designing Large Scale Web Sites: A Virtual Design Methodology 9
Dewey Decimal System 25, 27, 28, 29
Dilbert 24
DOS 11
Dowling, Thomas 6
Durrant, M. Gay 62

E-Mail xi, 23, 32, 35, 39, 40, 56, 78, 89, 90, 91, 92, 111, 112, 120
EDUCOM 121, 124
Edupage 124
EFFector Online 124, 125
Electronic Frontier Foundation (EFF) 95, 121–122, 124, 125
Emory University 56
Estrada, Susan xi
Evanston Public Library 18

FAQ (Frequently Asked Question) 95, 167–172
First Amendment *see* US Constitution
Flanders, Bruce 71–72, 148
Flint Public Library 18
Florida International University 55, 148
Freenet 111
FTP (File Transfer Protocol) 78, 82, 87, 89, 90, 92, 94
Funk, Evie 64

General Atomic 122
Georgia Institute of Technology 108
Gillespie, Dr. Thom 6, 149
Gopher xx, 56, 62, 78, 82, 87, 89, 90, 95
Gray, Matthew xviii

Habanero 107
HB1630 Computer or Telephone Network; transmitting misleading data (Georgia) 35–36
Henderson, Carole xix
Hert, Carol A. 88
High Performance Computing Act of 1991 32
Hill, Charles 65, 148
Hoffman, D.L. 33
Hopkins West Junior High School 64
Horton, W.M. 21
Houston Public Library 4–5
HTML and CGI Unleashed 2
HTML (Hypertext Markup Language) xi, xii, 9, 10, 11–16, 20, 44, 45, 84, 89, 97, 98, 99, 100, 101, 102, 107, 109, 116, 119, 175–176
  Anchor Tags 14
  Applets 15, 117
  Forms 10, 100
  Frames 15, 16, 97, 100, 175–176
  Image Maps 10, 16, 101
  Images 10, 14, 16, 21, 43, 44, 99
  Paired Tags 13
  Tables 15, 97
  Unpaired Tags 13
Huffman, Mike 59, 60
Hypertext xiii, xvi, 3, 10, 14, 17–19, 20

IBM xv
Icons xiii, 10, 21, 44
Indiana State Department of Education 59, 148
Indiana University 6, 18, 148
InfoMINE 26
Information Superhighway xvii, xx, 48
Information Technology (IT) xx
Ingram, Catherine E. 46
Intellectual Freedom xii, xiv, xxi, 2, 31–46, 49
  Access 43–44, 49

Content Rating Systems 31, 36, 37, 38
Filtering Software 31, 36, 37, 38, 70, 71, 72
Free Speech 31, 34, 39, 40
Intellectual Property 44–45
Privacy 31, 41–43, 78
Intellectual Freedom Manual 46
International Federation of Library Associations and Institutions 112, 148
Internet Chat 56, 117, 118
Internet Explorer xviii, 11, 16, 20, 22, 40, 90, 95, 96
Internet Public Library 41, 42, 118
Internet Scout Report 125
Internet Society xviii, 122
InterNIC 122, 125
Iowa State University 25
IP Address 62, 92
Ithaca College 101

Jackson, Christopher 6, 7, 8
Jakob, D. 83
Java 9, 10, 45, 107, 117, 121
Javascript 107
Johnson, Roberta 28
Journal of Performance and Instruction 21
Justie, Kevin 68, 149

Kalsbeck, W.D. 33
Kansas City Public Library 18
Kehoe, Brendan 93
Keller, C. 101
Kinneman, D. 46
Koch, T. 96, 97
Krug, Judith F. 46, 147

Lawrence Public Library 66, 71–73, 148
LeFurgy, B. 115
Leita, Carole 27, 69 148
Leonard, A. 83
Levine, Jenifer 24, 148
Libraries xvii, xviii, xx, xxi, xxii, 10, 32, 38–47, 50–79, 81, 102–105, 107, 110, 118–120
Academic xx, 6, 54–57
Public xix, xx, 6, 32, 36, 38, 40, 41, 44, 57–79, 81, 110, 112, 113
School xx, 32, 36, 38, 40, 41, 44, 57–79, 110, 112, 113
Library Bill of Rights 49, 64, 75, 76, 77, 79
Library of Congress 25, 26, 102
Lichtman, J. 100
Listproc 90, 91
Listserv 42, 48, 71, 90, 91, 92, 111, 120
Lynx 11, 15, 95, 96

Macintosh xv, 11
Madonna 71
Majordomo 90, 91
Manning, Bill 53
Maricopa Center for Learning and Instruction 98
Massachusetts Institute of Technology xviii
McClure, Charles R. xxi, 108
McKenzie, Jamieson 58–59, 147
McKiernan, Gerry 25
Meeker, M. 109
Microsoft xviii, 116, 117, 122–123
Microsoft Office 117
Microsoft Word 11
Miller, Steven E. 111
Minnesota Coalition Against Censorship (MCAC) 57–58, 148
Monroe County Community School District 59, 61, 148
Monroe County Public Library (MCPL) 6–9, 12
MOO (Multiuser Object Oriented environment) 42, 118
Morgan Stanley Company 109
Morin, G. 40
Morino Institute 111
Morton Grove Public Library (MGPL) 2, 4, 5, 27, 28, 49, 67, 68, 73, 149
Mosaic xvii, xviii, 11, 40, 90, 95, 96
Mount Arlington Public Library 5
Mundie, David 28

Napoli, Donald 71, 149
Nathaniel H. Wilson Middle School 24
National Center for Supercomputing Applications (NCSA) xvii

National Commission on Libraries and Information Sciences 108
National Information Infrastructure (NII) xix, xxi, 32, 44, 46, 48, 110, 111, 112
National Research Council 41
National Science Foundation (NSF) 31, 48
Neal-Schuman xi
Net-Happenings 125
Netcraft xviii
Netfind 93
Netscape xvii, xviii, 11, 15, 20, 22, 40, 64, 72, 90, 95, 96, 100, 116, 117, 123, 124
Netscout 122, 123
Network Solutions 122
Network Wizards xviii
New Castle Henry County Public Library 69–70
New York Times xvii
Newark Memorial High School 62–63, 149
News.Com 123
1996 National Survey of Public Libraries and the Internet xxi, 6
Northwestern College 96, 97
Novak, T.P. 33
NTIA Office of Telecommunications and Information Applications 46

O'Reilly & Associates xi
OCLC 28
Oregon Public Electronic Network (OPEN) 74

Pacific Lutheran University 94
Paul, K. 83
PC Magazine 99
Perkins, Don 53
Perl 10
Pico 11, 84
PINE 91
Platform for Internet Content Selection (PICS) 36, 107, 113, 124
Provo City Library 4
Putnam Valley School District 65

Quint, V. 117

Rand Corporation 112
Rau, Anne 50
Reading Public Library 23
Resnick, P. 36
Rezmierski, Virginia 72–73
Rice-Lively, M.L. 102
Robert A. L. Mortvedt Library 94
Rogers, S. 101
Rose, C. 100
Rose, Lance 48
Rosenbaum, Howard 85, 86, 98
Rosenfeld, Louis 24
Ruby, D. 115

Sackman, Gleason xx
Saint Joseph County Public Library 53, 68, 69, 70, 73, 149
St. Paul Public Library 17
Salcedo, M. R. 117
Salem Public Library 74
Sano, Darrell 9, 10
SBT Accounting 100
Schafer, Keith 29
Schneider, Karen xi
Schrock, Kathy 24, 149
Seattle Public Library 5
Seidman's Online Insider 125
Spokane Public Library 23, 27
Stull, Nina 62, 149
Sun Microsystems 123, 124
SURAnet 48
Surfwatch 70, 72

Telecommunications Act of 1996 *see* Communications Decency Act
Telnet xi, 78, 82, 87, 89, 90, 92, 93
Time Magazine 59
Training xii, xiv, xxi, 81–105, 163–165
  for Librarians 82–86, 101–102
  for Patrons 86–101
  templates 88–102

University of California, Riverside 26
University of Houston 55, 56, 149
University of Minnesota 95
University of Nevada Reno 95
Unix 84, 85, 91, 167

URL (Uniform Resource Locator) xvi, 14, 17, 19, 20, 37, 121
US Constitution 40, 41, 46, 54, 74, 75
US Department of Commerce xix
US Department of Defense xvii
US Department of Education 18, 60
US Department of Justice 114
US Environmental Protection Agency 18
US Supreme Court 74
USENET xi, 35, 37, 39, 42, 43, 78, 90, 91, 92, 120, 126

Veronica 95
Vi 84

Web4Lib 125–126
Webster, K. 83
WebTV 117
WEDNET 59
Werbach, Kevin 98, 149
Whitman, Mark 59, 60, 61
Whitmill, Glenna 70
Willard, Nancy 64
Williams College 54–55, 147
Windows xvii, 11
WordPerfect 11, 117
World Wide Web (WWW) xi, xii, xiii, xvi, xvii, xx, 3, 4, 6, 7, 9, 10, 15, 16, 17, 18, 25, 26, 27, 29, 31, 33, 36, 37, 40, 42, 43, 44, 45, 50, 55, 56, 57, 65, 67, 70, 78, 82, 83, 84, 85, 87, 89, 92, 95, 96, 97, 98, 102, 108, 114, 120, 121
  Browsers xii, xv, xvi, xvii, xviii, xx, 11, 13, 16, 22, 40, 45, 55, 87, 89, 90, 95, 96, 97, 104, 107, 109, 116, 119
  Pages xviii, 1–29, 35, 37, 38, 41, 42, 44, 45, 47, 49, 55, 61, 62, 67, 68, 69, 78, 81, 84, 89, 105, 116, 117, 123, 161–163
    Design xii, xiv, xxi, 1–29
      Color 20–21, 99
      Consistency 17–18
      Content 23–25
      Fonts 20
      Interactivity 23
      Navigational Cues 17–18
      Size 19–20
      Storyboarding 3
    Organization 3–9, 26–29
  Search Engines 82–83, 96, 97
World Wide Web Consortium 11, 15, 36, 96, 98, 100, 107, 113, 116, 124

Yahoo 27
Yale University 55

Zager, Carl 59, 61, 62, 148
Zen and the Art of the Internet 93
Zweizig, Douglas L. xxi, 108

About the Authors

Lisa Champelli worked as a writer and editor for an international service magazine before returning to school to pursue an interest in library services to children and the Internet. She received both her bachelor's degree in journalism and her master's degree in library and information science from Indiana University, Bloomington. Upon completing her MLS in May 1996, she had the wonderful good fortune to obtain a full-time position as a children's librarian at the Monroe County Public Library (MCPL) in Bloomington, where she spends her days promoting good books and information literacy skills to inquisitive kids. In addition to developing and maintaining MCPL's Children's Services Web site and various Web resource guides, she conducts the library's "Introduction to the Internet" workshops for both children and teachers, and always keeps an eye out for fun stories to tell.

Howard Rosenbaum joined the faculty of the School of Library and Information Science at Indiana University, Bloomington in 1993. His research interests include the history and development of electronic networking, with a focus on the emerging National Information Infrastructure and its implications for the information professions, the "public digital library," electronic commerce, electronic publishing and copyright, community networking, computer mediated communication, the study of managers, information, and organizations, and the intersection of theoretical approaches in library and information science and sociology. Rosenbaum has been a co-author on two national research studies, Managing Information Technologies: Transforming County Governments in the 1990s (1992), and The National Research and Education Network: Research and Policy and Perspectives (1991). He has presented his work at ASIS midyear and national meetings, the International Communications Association, the Canadian Association for Information Science, and the American Sociological Association.

Rosenbaum teaches in the areas of information networking, electronic commerce, intellectual freedom, information organizations, and social science information and offers continuing workshops for librarians and information professionals in HTML, Web page design, and the use of the Internet.